Samuel Boston Lathan

Grand Old Man, The Life of Samuel Boston Lathan

By S. Robert Lathan, Jr. M.D.
His Grandson

Published by
Wings Publishers
460 Ivy Park Lane
Atlanta, Georgia 30342

Text ©2012 by S. Robert Lathan, Jr., M.D.

Design and layout by Nicola Simmonds Carmack

All rights reserved. No part of this publication may be reproduced, stored in a retrieval system, or transmitted in any form or by any means — electronic, mechanical, photocopy, recording, or any other — except for brief quotations in printed reviews, without prior permission of the publisher.

Manufactured in the United States of America

10 9 8 7 6 5 4 3 2 1
First Edition

ISBN 978-1-930897-19-9

Foreword

Samuel Boston Lathan, my grandfather, was known as "Boss" and "Chester's Grand Old Man." He was Chester, South Carolina's, last surviving Confederate veteran.

At the Atlanta Civil War Roundtable, I would frequently overhear dinner table neighbors mentioning their great grandfathers who fought in the Civil War. I would interject that my *grandfather* actually fought in this war. Immediately they would question, "Surely you mean your great grandfather, don't you?" But I maintained to their amazement my truth, "No, I mean my grandfather!"

This apparently was some kind of record, but is explained by the fact that my father did not marry until the age of 49, and I was not born until he was 58. (Then my grandfather was 95.)

In all my years, I have encountered only three other individuals whose grandfathers fought in the Civil War. One was the late Dr. Harris Dew of Atlanta who was about twenty-five years older than me. Another man, Dave Matthews, owned a bike shop in Atlanta and introduced me to running at Kennesaw Mountain. (We also ran the New York City Marathon together.) But Dave's father, like mine, was way up in years before he was born, as he was the youngest of several siblings. The third was my friend and neighbor, Jim Herndon, of Kings Mountain, NC and Atlanta, whose grandfather William Andrew Mauney served in the NC regiments from Cleveland County and was later the county's first state representative in 1895.

Sadly, I was only one year old when my grandfather died at age 96. He was a self-educated man and had a lifelong quest for learning; like his brother, the Rev. Robert Lathan, he was known as a "Scribbler," and I have collected numerous "sketches" and articles that he wrote for the newspapers.

When I completed the JFK 50-Mile Ultramarathon in Maryland in 1984 I ran near the site of my grandfather's battle wounding. I went on to finish three more JFK races and was able to tour both Antietam and South Mountain battlefields. On one occasion, Mike Priest, a high school history teacher and author (an authority on the Battle of South Mountain) showed me exactly the site in the field where my grandfather was shot.

Foreword

In 2002 I published *The History of South Carolina*, a collection of the writings of my great uncle, the Reverend Robert Lathan, D.D., which described in detail the events of the Revolutionary War in South Carolina. Through the encouragement of my wife Millie, I began to research and review the clippings and articles that I had collected and could access on my own grandfather, the younger brother of the Rev. Robert Lathan.

After many years of gathering, it is with great pleasure that I can now publish the record of this remarkable man's life. This work was considerably enhanced by the numerous articles and photographs supplied by my cousin, Leila Stroud Welch of Birmingham, Alabama. Recognition is also due for the support of other cousins, George Harvey Moore and Ann Davidson Marion, both of Chester, SC.

Most importantly, I want to thank my wife Millie for her wonderful ideas and her unfailing support from day one, when she first suggested this project.

My special thanks to my publisher, Ginger Watkins for her encouragement and creativity, and without whose overall guidance this work would not have been possible.

Table of Contents

Foreword

Section One — Grand Old Man

    Chester's "Grand Old Man," Died Yesterday
    Chester Reporter "Funeral"
    Chester Reporter "Editorial"
    Samuel Boston Lathan
    Susan A. Meek
    Teaching, Work Career, and Other Interests
    Works Progress Administration Writers Project
    Lathan Genealogy "Tree"
    Children of Samuel Martin Lathan and Martha Patterson
    Children of Rev. Robert Lathan and Fannie Barron
    Children of Samuel Boston Lathan and Susan Amanda Meek
    Migration to America
    Robert Kilpatrick
    Samuel Martin Lathan and Martha Patterson
    Reverend Robert Lathan, D.D.
    Two Great Brothers
    Susie Meek Lathan
    Samuel Robert Lathan and Callie Mims Purvis
        S. Robert Lathan, Jr. M.D, Author
    Notable Editors in the Lathan Family
        Robert Lathan, Jr.
        Lapsey Barron Mills, Jr.
        David Lathan Mims
        Sandra Stovall Mims Rowe

Table of Contents

Lathan Family Cousins
    Leila Duva Nixon Babb
    George Harvey Moore
    Robert Edward Stroud
    Leila Caldwell Stroud Welch
    Augustus Theodore Allen, IV
    James Lathan Allen, M.D.
    George Ashley Allen

Family Letters
    Dr. Chalmers Davidson
    Mary Beth Purvis Howle
    Dr. William Pressly

Section Two — Chester County's Oldest Confederate Veteran

Official Confederate War Record
Timeline of War Record
Camps of the 17th South Carolina Regiment
S. B. Lathan's Written War Record
Samuel B. Lathan's Account of Wounding
Battle of South Mountain
John F. Kennedy Ultra Marathon
Sherman's Carolina Campaign
Sherman's Burning of Lathan Plantation
Introduction to Mount Pleasant Commissary
Henry Slade Tew Letters, Mount Pleasant
General Nathan G." Shanks" Evans
General Joe Johnston

Section Three — SBL Scribblings

- Mr. S. B. Lathan Had Quest for Learning
- Our Early Settlers
- Long Forgotten Worthies
- Blackstock Reminiscences
- The Old Time Militia
- The Textile Industry
- Hopewell A.R.P. Church
- The U.C.V. Dinner
- Judge Thos. J. Mackey
- Sketch of Judge John Hemphill
- From Ancient Courthouse Records
- Fourth of July at Caldwell's
- Civil War Veteran Tells Story of Submarine
- McConnellsville
- Godfather of York
- The War of the 60's
- How Dr. Saml. B. Lathan Spent Christmas
- The Seventeenth S. C. V
- Mr. S. B. Lathan Talks Interestingly
- W.W. Dixon Has A Talk With Mr. S. B. Lathan
- Address and Reminiscences
- The Chester Reporter, October 1938
- Historical Sketches of Chester County

Section Four — A Willingness to Help

- Acknowledgements

Section One

Grand Old Man

Dr. Samuel B. Lathan, Chester's "Grand Old Man," Died Yesterday

The Chester Reporter
March 9, 1939

Dr. Samuel Boston Lathan, the last Chester county Confederate veteran, who would have been ninety-seven years of age, had he been privileged to live until May 2nd, died yesterday morning at 7:15 o'clock at his home on Saluda street. For several days he had been losing ground, and it had been evident that the end was but a matter of short time.

Dr. Lathan was one of this section's most distinguished sons, and was frequently referred to as Chester county's first citizen. The degree of Doctor of Letters was conferred upon him by Erskine College for his scholarship, and for his outstanding interest in all matters educational. He had been a resident of the city of Chester 67 years. Possessing a distinguished record in his four years service in the War Between the States he was always greatly interested in the Confederate cause. Up to the very last he possessed a remarkably clear and accurate memory. He had written widely on many historical subjects. His mind was a vast store house of information and he was always glad to furnish information to people.

Dr. Lathan is survived by four children: Mrs. Robert B. Caldwell, James M. Lathan, Miss Susie Lathan, and Samuel Robert Lathan, all of Chester, six grand-children and four great grand-children. He married Miss Susan A. Meek on October 22, 1874. She died in September, 1924.

Dr. Lathan was a son of the late Samuel Martin Lathan and the late Martha Patterson Lathan of the Blackstock section of Fairfield county, having been born May 2, 1842.

He received his education at the A.C. Elder school at Blackstock. He prepared himself to pursue a course in law at the College of South Carolina, now the University of South Carolina, however the war cut short his plans.

Dr. Lathan witnessed four years of brilliant service in the Confederate army. He early joined the Confederate colors, uniting with Company D, Seventeenth South Carolina regiment. He saw extensive service in most of the Southern states. The regiment was initially dispatched to the South Carolina coast. In May, 1862, the regiment was sent to Virginia. His regiment was engaged in a battle at Malvern Hill, Va. Following this engagement the 17th regiment joined the initial Maryland campaign.

Dr. Lathan was in the thick of the fighting at Sharpsburg, Md. at Second Manassas and at Rappahannock.

At South Mountain, Md. in the terrific battle, Dr. Lathan suffered a wound in his thigh and he was left on the battlefield. Shortly afterwards he was taken prisoner to Frederick City, Md., and then to Baltimore, Md. for three months. During January, 1863, he was exchanged and rejoined the famous 17th regiment at Wilmington, NC, and marched with the regiment to Charleston, SC and remained there on James Island for awhile. Then the regiment was dispatched to Mississippi and was in the heavy fighting outside of Vicksburg. After the Unionists captured Vicksburg, his regiment fell back and marched to Jackson, Miss., where there was heavy fighting for 10 days. The regiment was then sent to Savannah, Ga., then to Charleston, SC and from there to Petersburg, Va., and he was at Greensboro, NC when the war ended.

With the war ended he returned home and started teaching school near Blackstock. After teaching there one year, Dr. Lathan taught for two years, where Gastonia, NC is now located. He then taught for three years at McConnellsville, and one year at Blairsville. He was elected principal of the Vineville, Ga., school, but ill health ended his teaching career and he moved to Chester on September 1, 1872 and began his business career.

He first became book-keeper for the large general mercantile business of Wylie, Roddey & Agura, remaining there for three years. He then became book-keeper for George Melton, a prominent cotton factor, staying there during 1875. Next he became local agent for the Richmond & Danville Railway for three years. Dr. Lathan resigned this work to become partner in W. Holmes Harden & Co. He stayed with this firm until it was dissolved about 1884.

Dr. Lathan then entered the cotton business, where he became a prominent factor. He retired from the business in 1889 and became secretary and treasurer of the former Chester Gingham Mills and the Catawba Mill, remaining in this capacity until the plants were purchased by the late Col. Leroy Springs. He then re-entered the cotton business in which he became an outstanding cotton factor of Chester. He retired from this business many years ago.

He was the oldest Royal Arch Mason in South Carolina.

Dr. Lathan had taught Sunday School for 64 years. Sixty years at the Chester Associate Reformed Presbyterian church and four years at other places.

He took a deep interest in the Chester, A.R.P. church being an elder.

Dr. Lathan was also greatly interested in Erskine College.

He had planned to write a history of the Red Shirt era, with which he was very familiar.

In addition to his four children already mentioned, Dr. Lathan leaves a sister, Mrs. M. A. Garvin, of Hartsville.

The Funeral

The funeral service was held at the A.R.P. church at 11 A.M. today, with the pastor, Dr. Joseph L. Grier, in charge, assisted by Dr. John McSween. In deference to Dr. Lathan's views and the family's wishes, the service was very simple, consisting of selections from the Scriptures, prayers by the ministers, and two numbers by the choir.

The pall-bearers were Messrs. M.H. White, Jake S. Colvin, H. R. Woods, M. G. Sandifer, Jas. M. Robinson, J.S. Caldwell, James I. Hardin, and Edward M. White.

Officers of the church and friends were honorary pall-bearers.

Business was suspended in Chester during the funeral of this distinguished and beloved citizen.

Chester Reporter Editorials March 9, 1939

Dr. Samuel B. Lathan

Dr. Samuel B. Lathan, who passed peacefully away yesterday morning at his home in this city, had not only attained an age attained by very few, and was not only the last of the Chester county lads in gray who marched away so blithely those early spring days in 1861-he was more than that. He was an institution. His age, his almost inexhaustible store of information, his philosophic outlook, his matured judgment all combined to make him a community asset.

How many times has the expression been used, "Ask Mr. Lathan?" He was expected to have the required information, and generally did. His knowledge embraced many subjects, and to the last he continued his studies and reading. To him Chester county is indebted for the preservation of much of its history; and it's a thousand pities that some step was not taken while there was yet time to have him put into print all that he knew pertaining to the history of this section.

All who knew Dr. Lathan know, of course, that he was a Christian gentleman in all that expression implies, and his service as a teacher in the Sabbath School for more than sixty years, his interest in the Lord's work, and his extensive knowledge of the Scriptures speak as to that.

Dr. Lathan's greatest contribution, perhaps, next to his services as a churchman, was, perhaps, to education. Belonging to that group, "Who gave their merry youth away for country and for God."

Dr. Lathan had not allowed great cataclysm to wreck his life. After four years of hardship and adventure, he returned to South Carolina to take up the tattered ends of life, resolved to carry out his plans as nearly as possible. Circumstances forbade to a certain extent, but they could not prevent the spirited youth from pressing toward, and eventually attaining, the goal he had set. He became a scholar, a man of vast erudition, a man whose judgment and opinion were regarded as final. And it was his services to the cause of education in the days when there was no public school system in South Carolina that probably marked his greatest contribution as a citizen. He participated actively in the movement in Chester many years ago that gave this community one of the first graded school systems in the State, and served on the County Board of Education when the office was little more than a name. But a movement had been started, and out of that beginning finally emerged what we have today.

Young men by the score and, perhaps, young women, too, of an earlier day were prepared for entrance examinations, scholarship examinations, and other competitive tests by this man, whose own opportunities had been very limited, owing to the lack of schools in his day, and the intervention of the cruel war which had sent so many a fine young man to death, and brought down in ruins the plans of so many others. But this exceptional and most extraordinary man had conquered circumstances, and persistence and determination had won him all that circumstances might have denied.

All will miss Dr. Lathan — his benign personality, his inspiring presence, his profound store of information, his love of his fellow-man, and his never-failing willingness to help. But let us thank God that we were privileged to have such a man sojourn in out midst for all of these years, to be the great blessing and inspiration that he was, and seek to emulate his example, and pattern our lives, as far as we are able, after this.

Photograph of the portrait of Samuel Boston Lathan. Original portrait was in the home on Saluda Street in Chester, SC. Now portrait is in the home of Dr. James Allen in Blowing Rock, NC.

Samuel Boston Lathan 1842–1939

Samuel Boston Lathan in his 30's

The son of Samuel Martin Lathan and Martha Patterson was born May 2, 1842, in Blackstock, Fairfield County, South Carolina.

He was educated in the Blackstock schools leaving his university plans to join the South Carolina militia to fight in the Civil War. He made a miraculous recovery from being wounded at the Battle of South Mountain during the Antietam Campaign in 1862. For seven years after the War, he taught school in several communities, returning to Chester in 1872.

Mr. Lathan married Susan Amanda Meek October 22, 1874 and together raised four children: Leila Hope Lathan, James Martin Lathan, Susie Meek Lathan, and Samuel Robert Lathan. Most of their lives they lived in the same home on Saluda Street in Chester.

Mr. Lathan worked mainly as a cotton factor in Chester as well as being an active teacher in the Associate Reformed Presbyterian church. One of his great pleasures was what he called "scribbling" as he both spoke and wrote of the history of the community and his role as a member of the 17th South Carolina Infantry Regiment.

Dr. Lathan received an honorary Doctor of Literature from Erskine College in 1934.

He died March 8, 1939 at age 96 and is buried in Evergreen Cemetery, Chester, SC.

Susan Amanda Meek 1845-1924

Susan Amanda Meek in her 30's

The wife of Samuel Boston Lathan was born Sept. 27, 1845, in Louisville, Mississippi. She was the daughter of James Byers Meek and Cornelia Laura Rainey of York County, SC. Susan Meek returned to York County after the death of her father in 1854 and made her home in Brattonsville, SC, until Mrs. Meek married Robert S. Hope. Then Susan moved to Lowrys, SC.

She attended Yorkville Female Seminary and later graduated from Columbia Female College. She married Samuel Boston Lathan in 1874 and lived in Chester, SC. They had two daughters, Leila and Susie Meek and two sons, James and Samuel Robert.

Her great grandfather on her mother's side, Samuel Rainey, was a signer of the SC Ordinance of Secession.

She died at age 79 in 1924.

Samuel Boston Lathan

Teaching, Work Career, Church and other Interests

Prior to the Civil War, Samuel Boston Lathan received his education at the A. C. Elder School at Blackstock. He prepared himself to pursue a course in law at the College of South Carolina, now the University of South Carolina. However, the war cut short his plans.

After the War, he started teaching school at Blackstock for one year, then for two years where Gastonia, North Carolina is now located, then for three years at McConnellville in York County, and one year at Blairsville, Georgia. He ended his teaching career as a school principal at Vineville, Georgia (a section of Macon) but left at age 30 to return to Chester, South Carolina, on September 1, 1872, to begin his business career.

He was first a bookkeeper for the large general mercantile business of Wylie, Roddey, and Agurs. After three years he became a bookkeeper for George Melton, a prominent cotton factor. Next he became the lead agent for the Richmond and Danville Railway for three years. He resigned this work to become a partner in W. Holmes Harden & Co., staying with this firm until it was dissolved in 1884.

Entering the cotton business next, he became a prominent cotton factor for several years until retiring in 1889 to become the secretary and treasurer of the former Chester Gingham Mills and the Catawba Mill, until the plants were purchased by Col. Leroy Springs. Finally he reentered the cotton business and was again an outstanding cotton factor in Chester, South Carolina. In 1920, after retiring from cotton, he was manager of the Chester County Farmer's Warehouse Co. He took a deep interest in the Chester A.R.P. Church, serving as ruling elder and teaching Sunday School for over sixty years. He was the oldest Royal Arch Mason in South Carolina and was greatly interested in Erskine College. He was a member of the "Chautauqua Society," the first literary society in Chester.

Mr. Lathan was still very active in the Chester community in his 90's.

Section One — Grand Old Man

Samuel Boston Lathan and Susan Meek in later life.

Samuel Boston and Susan Meek were buried in Evergreen Cemetery in Chester, SC.

Dr. Samuel B. Lathan
96 Years Old
W. W. Dixon

**Works Progress Administration
Writers Project Interview
June 28, 1938
Winnsboro, SC
Project #1655**

Dr. Samuel Boston Lathan is the oldest white citizen of Chester County, South Carolina. He lives with an unmarried daughter, Miss Susie Lathan, in a handsome two-story residence on Saluda Street, near the U. S. Post Office in the town of Chester, S. C. He owns the place and is one of the outstanding citizens of the community. By reason of strength, he has attained the Biblical allotment of four score years and ten and exceeded it by sixteen years; yet, from the erectness of his carriage, the texture of his skin, and the timbre of his voice, one would never think that he was a man of that age.

"Well, it will give me pleasure to talk to you of what I remember of life from 1848 to 1938. You know I can't remember when I was born, but that event was recorded by my mother as having taken place on the 2nd day of May, 1842 about three miles southeast of Blackstock, SC in Fairfield County. My father was a farmer, Samuel M. Lathan. My mother before marriage was Martha Patterson. The result of this marriage was five boys and six girls. I suppose the most distinguished one of the family was my older brother, Robert born in 1829. He received his education at Erskine College, became a teacher, a school commissioner of York County, and a minister of the Gospel in the Associate Reformed Presbyterian Church. His son, Robert, was editor of the *Charleston News and Courier* and, later, the Asheville *Citizen*.

"I began my education in an old field school near our home, taught by Mr. William Douglass. I was six years old then. All small children commenced in the old blue-backed speller. Beginners paid ten dollars per scholastic year of eight months. When we reached the grammar grades, the tuition was fifteen dollars. In the advanced grades, including Latin and Greek, the tuition was twenty-five dollars. The school hours were from 8 a.m. until 6 p.m. There was an intermission of one hour for dinner and recreation. We carried water from a nearby spring. On a shelf in the schoolroom was a wooden bucket containing drinking water. A drinking gourd hung on a nail above the bucket. It was quite a privilege to get permission to go to the spring for a bucket of fresh water during school hours. Our teacher was a Presbyterian and believed in the proverb, "Spare the rod and spoil the child." The people of the community had great confidence in his learning, probity, and executive ability. Usually a whipping at school was followed by a sound thrashing at home, for good measure.

"At recess the large boys played catball, and the younger boys and girls played antony-over, marbles, and rolley-holey. April the 1st was dreaded by most rural school teachers. The pupils would get inside and bar the teachers out. The teacher, who didn't act on the principle that discretion is the better part of valor, generally got the worst of it. Mr. Douglass soon learned this, and, on April Fool's Day, he would walk to the school, perceive the situation, laughingly announce there would be no school until the morrow, and leave. Our teacher required all pupils to study out loud. There was a pandemonium of spoken words going on all day in the school. Why did he require this? Well, it was to assure himself that no student was listlessly looking on his or her book and that everyone was busy. Every Friday afternoon we had a trapping spelling bee from the blue-backed speller. In this school we studied Smith's Grammar, Goff's Arithmetic, Morse's Geography, and Peter Parley's history. On the first Saturday in May, the school children went in wagons to Great Falls to a picnic and seined for shad. The Catawba River teemed with shad in those days.

"The Fourth of July was observed at Caldwell Cross Roads. The military companies of infantry would assemble here from the surrounding counties making up a brigade. A drill and inspection were had, and a dress parade followed. There was an old cannon mounted on the field. The honor of firing it was assigned to Hugh Reed, who had been in the artillery of Napoleon's army at Waterloo and afterward emigrated to South Carolina.

"A great barbecue and picnic would be served; candidates for military, state, and national offices would speak, hard liquor would flow, and each section would present its 'bully of the woods' in a contest for champion in a fist and skull fight. Butting, biting, eye gouging, kicking, and blows below the belt were barred. It was primitive prize fighting. I recall that a man names McGill won the belt. He was beaten the following year by Smith Harden.

"After crops were laid by, a great deal of visiting took place among the neighbors. The men inspected each other's crops and sumptuous dinners and watermelon feasts were exchanged. There was more neighborliness in the country then than now. Everybody went to church on the Sabbath, and children knew by rote the Shorter Catechism. Nearly every home in our community had family worship night and morning.

"There's something I now call to mind as strange. Funerals were never conducted inside of the churches. The ceremonial rites took place at the grave. Yes, I am a surviving Confederate soldier. I was a member of Capt. W. C. Beaty's company, in Governor John Hugh Means' regiment. I was wounded in the battle of South Mountain (Antietam). I was carried a prisoner of war to Baltimore. That was the conclusion of so much that was important in my military career.

"When I was a boy, my home town was Blackstock, named for its first postmaster, Edward Blackstock. The boundary line separating Chester and Fairfield counties runs through the center of town. Sometimes the post office is in Fairfield and sometimes in Chester. Now the line runs right through the post office, Kennedy's store. I have lived through the following wars in which my country has been engaged: The Mexican War, the War Between the States, the Spanish-American War, and the World War. I have been a constituent of the following Congressmen: W.W. Boyce, W. H. Perry, A. S. Wallace, John H. Evins, J. J. Hemphill, T. F. Strait, D. E. Finley, Stanyame Wilson, Joseph Johnson, W. H. Stevenson, Gen. John Bratton, Paul McCorkle, and the present one, J. P. Richards.

" I do not consider the military occupation and rule of South Carolina, just after the Civil War, unwise or oppressive. The county was demoralized. Disbanded soldiers, Confederates and Federals passing through the State, would have raided the homes of the residents and taken off every mule, horse, and ox, and left them without means of tilling the soil. The provost marshal of this district was Capt. Livingston. I never joined the Ku Klux. Yes, there were shortages of food and clothing during the war. Molasses was a substitute for sugar, parched meal and parched ground okra seed were used for coffee; and sassafras roots were used to make tea. Flour and meal sacks were made into men's, women's and children's clothing.

"The radical, carpetbag, scalawag government was inconceivably rotten and corrupt. An executive pardon could be bought and stealings were put through the legislature by appropriations and issuance of fraudulent bonds. Under the Constitution of 1865, judges were allowed to state and comment upon the facts and to disclose their opinion of what the verdict of a jury should be. This opinion could be and often was bought with money or its equivalent. A wealthy litigant had three chances: a bribed jury, a bribed circuit judge, and a bribed Supreme Court. A criminal had four chances, the ones I've just mentioned and a bribed governor, who could give him a pardon.

"One of the most interesting political characters evolved in this cess-pool of iniquitous politics was Judge T. J. Mackey. Born in Lancaster County, of poor parents, he went with them at an early age to Charleston, SC. By native ability, he won a beneficiary scholarship to the Citadel, the military college of South Carolina. He was a member of the Palmetto Regiment, and he fought through the Mexican War. In the War Between the States, he was an officer on the staff of General Sterling Price at the close of the war. When the carpetbaggers and Negroes got possession of the State government, he became a scalawag. Bright, witty, forceful, and with a veneer of good breeding, he was rewarded with the position of Judge of the 6th Circuit, and he resided right here in Chester. He was a conspicuous figure on our streets for years. Solomon in all his glory was no better arrayed. He wore broadcloth, Prince Albert coats, silk vests, checked trousers, and tall, silk, top hats, and carried gold-headed canes. During court week, he would have the sheriffs attend him with cocked hat and drawn sword preceeded by the bailiffs crying stentoriously, 'Give way! Give way! The Honorable Court is approaching!' He conducted the court proceedings with great pomp, magnificence, and dignity. The suspense of all this dignity was sometimes relieved by his wit and humor from the bench. In his inimitable manner he once addressed the grand jury of Fairfield County at Winnsboro in these words: 'Mr. Foreman and gentlemen of the grand inquest of the county. In addition to what I have already charged, you might extend your investigations into the hotels and boarding houses of Winnsboro and observe the martyrs at their 'steaks,' and also ascertain whether or not certain domestic animals, better known as bedbugs, are entitled to draw pensions from the U. S. Government on account of having drawn blood from the British soldiers while they were quartered here in the war of the Revolution.'

"On one occasion Mr. Lindsay, a reputable citizen of Chester, knocked a drunken politician down and was prosecuted in the court for assault and battery with intent to kill. Mr. Lindsay's attorney approached the judge with an idea of finding out what the sentence would be, provided the defendant would plead guilty. Mackay replied, 'You can safely leave the matter to me, sir.'

"When the plea was accepted by the solicitor and read by the clerk, all eyes and ears of the expectant court room* were turned on the judge. He said: 'Let the defendant, Lindsay, stand up. You have been charged in this indictment with an attempt to kill your fellow man. It's not your mercy that the prosecutor is not lying somewhere today in some silent graveyard. I could impose on you the maximum sentence of fifteen years at hard labor in the State penitentiary, but as you have saved the State some expense by your pleas of guilty, the sentence of this august court is that you, William Lindsay, be confined in the State penitentiary at hard labor for a period of ten years (dramatic pause) or pay a fine of one dollar."

*As in the original typed document

Sources:
Writers Project Interview: Library of Congress, Manuscript Division, WPA Federal Writers' Project

Soldiers Record, S. B. Lathan, National Archives, Washington, D.C.

Proceedings of Southern Historical Society; Prince William County Public Library, Bull Run Branch, Manassas, Virginia.

Family Records, held by George Moore of Chester, SC and William C. Lathan, Jr. of Triangle, Virginia

Lathan Genealogy "Tree"

James Lathan ┐
             ├─ Robert Lathan ┐
Peggy Waugh ─┘ 1759-1842   │
                              ├─ Samuel Martin Lathan
                Nancy Martin ─┘   1797-1890
                1766-1829

                              Robert Patterson ┐
                              1766-1855   │
Robert Kilpatrick ┐   ├─ Martha Patterson
1735-1840   ├─ Sarah Kilpatrick ─────────┘   1809-1890
                  │ 1778-1855
Isabella Dunn ────┘
1740-1825

Adam Meek ────┐
1725-1767   ├─ James Meek ┐
              │ 1758-1819 │
Jane Mitchell ┘   ├─ James Byers Meek
1730-1797   │   1810-1854
              Susannah Byers┘
              1771-1844

              Samuel Rainey ┐
              1789-1867   │
                            ├─ Cornelia Laura Rainey
                            │   1821-1892
              Lethea Beckham┘
              1797-1835

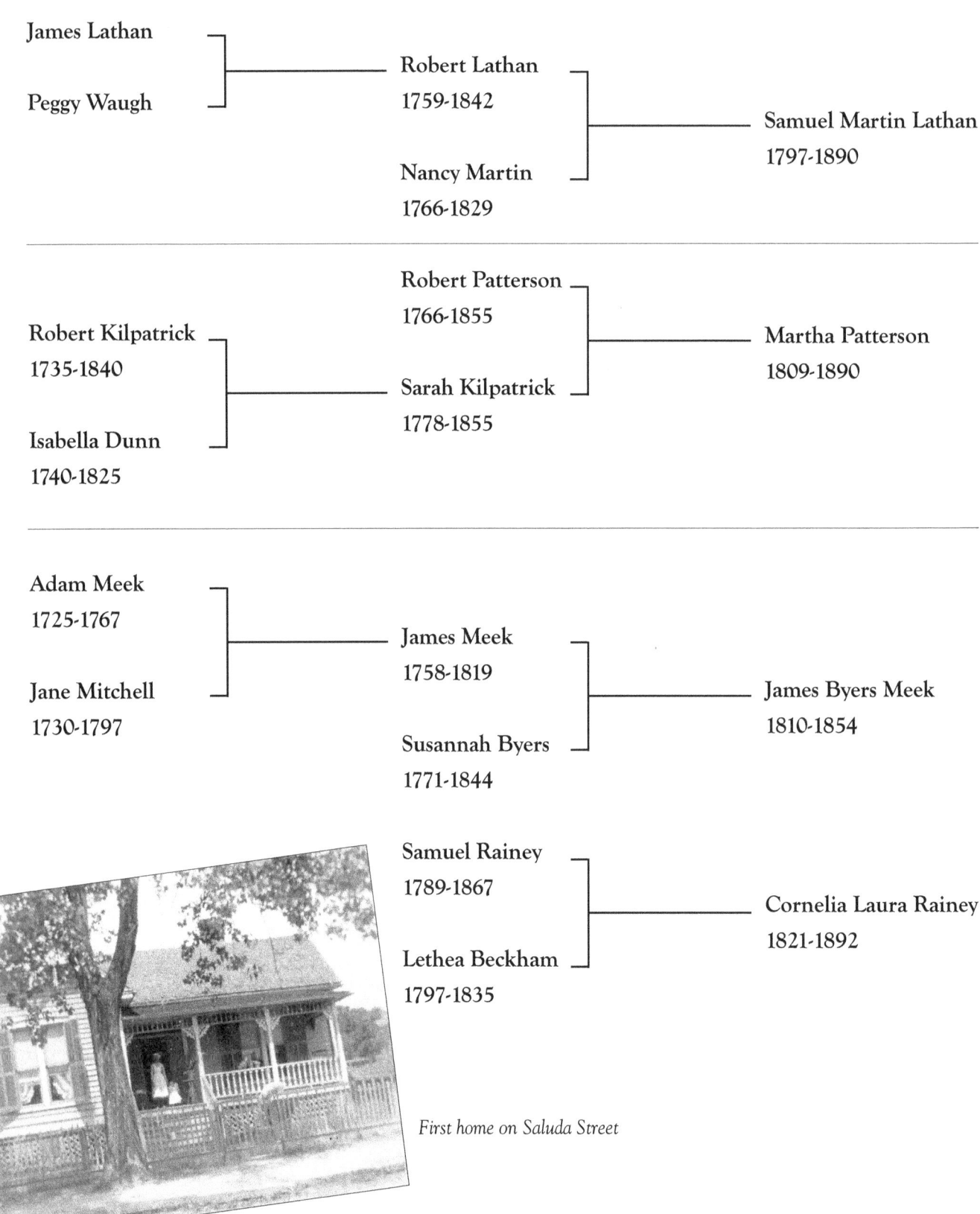

First home on Saluda Street

Eleven children including:

Rev. Robert Lathan
1829-1896

* Samuel Boston Lathan
1842-1939

Susan Amanda Meek
1845-1924

Leila Hope Lathan
1875-1967

James Martin Lathan
1877-1954

Susie Meek Lathan
1879-1958

Samuel Robert Lathan
1880-1942

Caroline Mims Purvis
1899-1981

** Samuel Robert Lathan, Jr.
1938 —

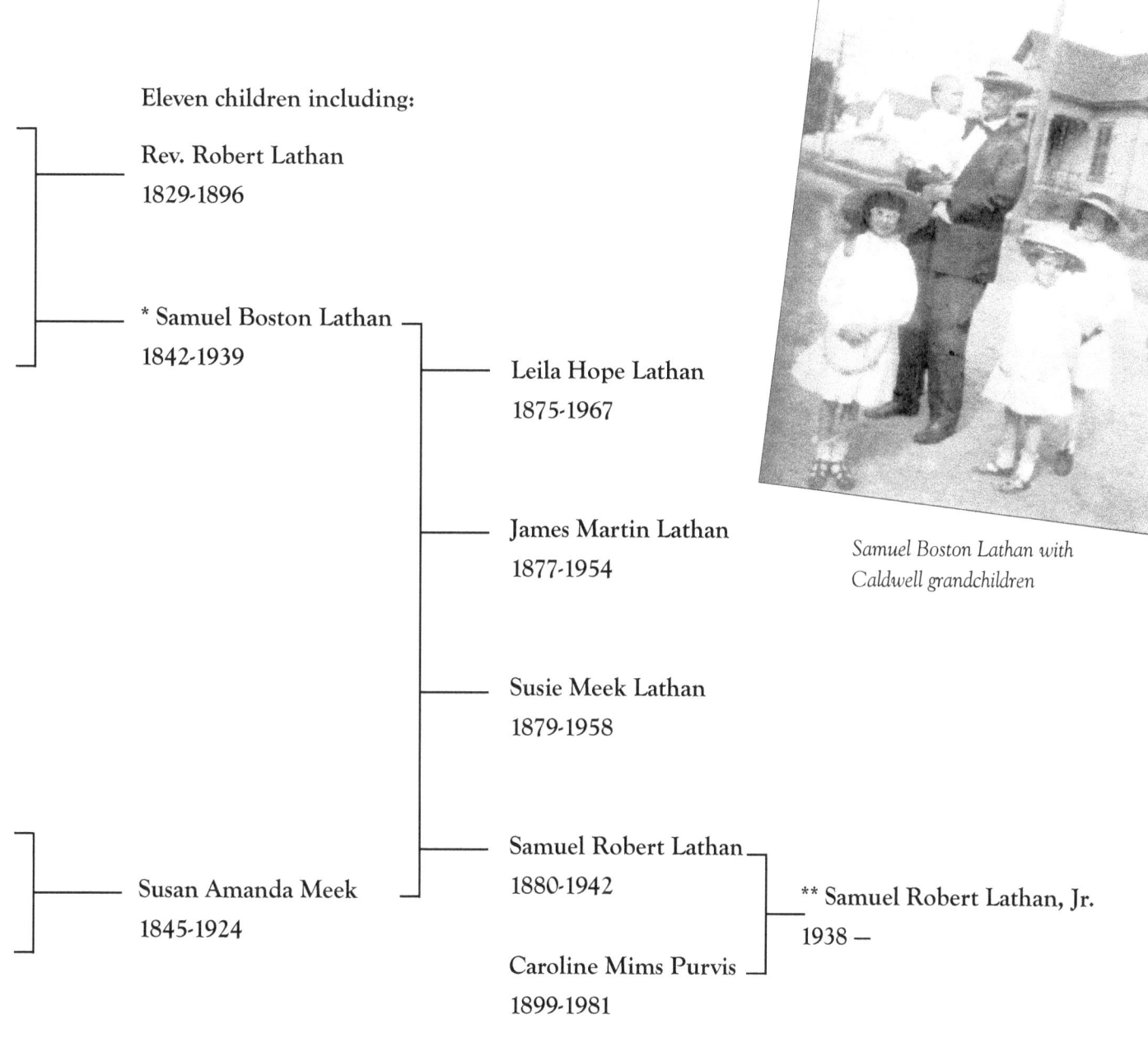

Samuel Boston Lathan with Caldwell grandchildren

* The subject — SBL
** The author — SRL, Jr.

Samuel Martin Lathan 1797-1890 and Martha Patterson 1809-1890

Eleven Children including
Rev. Robert Lathan 1829-1896
Nancy Martin Lathan 1831-1906
Sarah Kilpatrick Lathan 1833-1889
Mary Isabella Lathan 1836-1862
Sarah Jane Lathan 1838-1878
William James Lathan 1840-1927
Samuel Boston Lathan* 1842-1939
Martha Edith Lathan 1845-1929
John Brown Lathan 1847-1922
Margaret Ann Lathan 1850-1940
David Warren Lathan 1854-1908

Reverend Robert Lathan 1829-1896 and Fannie Barron 1838-1899

Seven Children
Samuel Boston Lathan 1862-1929 married Josephine Fischer 1866-1928
    Archie Ingram Lathan 1887
    Karl Patterson Lathan 1892
    Mathilde Dodelle Lathan 1896
    Robert Lathan 1899

Anna Isabel Lathan 1865-1903 married Rev. Thomas Bonner Stewart 1857-1940
    John Lathan Stewart 1888-1960 married Mamie Stewart
        Anne Lathan Stewart died in infancy
    Ruth Stewart 1890-1964 married Rev James Hunter Snell
        Five Children
    Charles Todd Stewart 1892-1960 married Leonor Pereira DeMagalhaes 1893-1921
        Charles Todd Stewart, Jr 1922
        Anna Louisa Stewart 1923
        Thomas Bonner Stewart 1924
        Edward Charles Pereira Stewart 1924
        Richard Hamilton Stewart 1928

Mary Amelia Lathan 1867-1933 married Warner Henry Whisonant 1856-1943
    Eugene Douglas Whisonant 1892
    Barron Henry Whisonant 1884
    Margaret Isabella Whisonant 1897
    Warren Henry Whisonant 1904

Nannie B. Lathan 1869-1913 married John Pinkney Mills 1851-1940
    12 children including
    Robert Lathan Mills 1897
        Robert L. Mills, Jr 1927
    Lapsey Barron Mills 1901
        Lapsey Barron Mills, Jr. 1927

Archibold Ingram Lathan 1871-died in infancy

Emma Martha Lathan 1875 married Oscar Lamar
    Four children

Robert Lathan, Jr. 1881-1937 married Bessie Agnes Early

Samuel Boston Lathan 1842-1939 and Susan Amanda Meek 1845-1924*

Four Children
Leila Hope Lathan 1875-1967 married Robert A. Caldwell 1874-1955
    Mary Simons Caldwell 1902-1990 married Drury Mealing Nixon 1901-1981
        Leila Duva Nixon 1926
    Leila Lathan Caldwell 1903-1992 married Coy Franklin Stroud 1905-1986
        Robert Edward Stroud 1934
        Leila Caldwell Stroud 1937
    Susie Meek Caldwell 1905-1991
    Robert Brice Caldwell, Jr. 1909-1991 married Ruth Eleanor Talton 1918-1995
        Eleanor Talton Caldwell 1944
        Robert Brice Caldwell III 1948

James, Susie, Robert, Leila

Samuel Boston Lathan

First row, left to right: Susie Meek, Susan Meek Lathan, Samuel Robert, Samuel Boston.
Second row, Leila Hope, James Martin

James Martin Lathan 1877-1959 married Georgia Morrall Ashley 1876-1958
    Anne Ashley Lathan 1908-1993 married Augustus Theodore Allen III 1899-1982
        Augustus Theodore Allen IV 1937
        James Lathan Allen 1939
        George Ashley Allen 1943

Susie Meek Lathan 1879-1958

Samuel Robert Lathan 1880-1942 married Caroline Mims Purvis 1899-1981
    Samuel Robert Lathan, Jr 1938 married Mary A. Hudson 1941**
        CarolineMims Lathan 1967
        Marion Stewart Lathan 1969
        Samuel Robert Lathan III 1975

Migration to America — The "Scotch-Irish"

From the time of King James I of England in 1605, a great many people from Scotland sought refuge in Northern Ireland (Ulster) to escape religious persecution. King James made Northern Ireland his "water plantation" in 1610. Most of these "Scotch-Irish" (also known as "Scots-Irish") were Presbyterians. A split occurred among those persecuted, with some known as Reformed Presbyterians or Covenanters.

The earliest known ancestral Lathan (also spelled Leathen) to emigrate from Scotland to County Antrim in Northern Ireland was James Lathan. He married Peggy Waugh and together they had five sons and three daughters. Three of the sons, David, William and Robert, emigrated to the United States leaving Belfast, Ireland, in 1788. The passage took nine weeks.

Their reason for leaving consisted of not only religious matters but also the economic deprivation with the collapse of the linen industry.

Upon arrival in Charleston, SC, in December, 1788, the three brothers went their separate ways: David to Genesee County, New York, and William and Robert to Williamsburg County in South Carolina. Robert, born in 1759, brought his wife Nancy Agnes Martin (whom he married in Ireland) with him to South Carolina.

A year after arriving in Charleston, Robert's family moved to Lancaster County and finally settled in Fairfield County, SC, in the Wateree Section near what is now known as White Oak. Land deed records show that in 1796, Robert purchased 150 acres in Fairfield County for 50 pounds sterling. In 1812 he petitioned for and received citizenship in the United States. Five of his children attained maturity: Sarah, John, William, Nancy, and Samuel. He gained additional land and eventually sold 188 acres to each son.

After his wife died in 1840, Robert moved to Tennessee to live with his daughter. He was buried there in Salem Cemetery, Tipton County, Tennessee, in 1842.

Two Families Migrate to America

James Lathan ⟶ Robert Lathan ⟶ Samuel Martin Lathan ⟶

Samuel Boston Lathan

Robert Kilpatrick ⟶ Sarah Kilpatrick ⟶ Martha Patterson ⟶

Samuel Boston Lathan

Robert Kilpatrick
1735–1840

The grandfather of Samuel Martin Lathan was born August 2, 1735, in County Antrim, Northern Ireland. He married Isabella Dunn and in 1760, had to flee the country "on account of his activities against the accouchement of the King of England upon the religious and political freedom of the people of North Ireland."

He and his wife came to America and settled in Fairfield County, SC. At the outbreak of the Revolutionary War he enlisted in the Continental Army. He served several tours during the entire war. Robert Kilpatrick, or as he was familiarly called, Bob Kilpatrick, is regarded as one of the first "fighting Irishmen." The luck of the Irish came to his rescue, each of the three times he escaped the British hangman's noose.

The following sketch of Robert Kilpatrick, a Revolutionary hero, was written by the Reverend Robert Lathan, D.D. and was found among his papers.

He came to America some years before the breaking out of the Revolutionary war. The precise time is not certainly known, perhaps it was in 1775, and settled in Fairfield county, South Carolina, near the headwaters of Wateree creek, afterwards moved to Chester county, South Carolina, and settled on the road from Chesterville to Winnsboro, within a few yards of the spot on which Hopewell church now stands. He was an Irishman and the tradition is that he was forced to fly from his native country on account of a rebellion into which he and some others had entered against some of the king's officers.

He and his party had met one night that they might concert plans for action, when, to their surprise, the house in which they were, was surrounded by the king's troops. Kilpatrick and his party were seated at a table, on which a single candle was burning. One of their number was writing and the rest were making suggestions. Without a moment's warning the door was broken open and the party were in the hands of an armed band of soldiers. The door was guarded, and after an examination of the company by the soldiers, it was decided to hang the whole of them on the spot. Ropes were put around their necks, and death by the halter began to stare the rebels in the face.

The house, it seems, was small, and the soldiers having rushed in stood on the side next to the door, whilst Kilpatrick saw it was but death anyway, and he determined to escape or die in the attempt. Being a vey large man, and also a man of great strength, he first blew out the light and then made a plunge amongst the king's troops, running over some and knocking others down, he opened a path to the door and leaped out into the darkness. The rest of the party followed, and all, in the confusion and darkness, escaped.

For a considerable time Kilpatrick kept himself concealed. Finally he determined to come to America. What little money he had was put into a belt, and fastened around the person of his wife beneath her clothes. This was done from the fear that he might be captured by the government officers and lose both his money and life. By prudent management, Kilpatrick and his family were enabled to get away from Ireland. Still, he was in continual dread during the passage of eight weeks, lest he should be seized, put in irons and sent back to Ireland to be tried, condemned and executed. With a heart full of joy he set his feet upon the shores of America in the city of Charleston. When the Revolutionary was broke out, he, without a moment's hesitation espoused with all of his heart the cause of the Whigs. The care of the family was committed wholly to his wife. Unfortunately for her, their homes, both in Fairfield and Chester, were hard by a nest of Tories. These were a class of persons who could not be said to be friends of the British government, but a set of heartless monsters, who banded together to plunder the Whig women in the absence of their husbands. Mrs. Kilpatrick spent a kind of migratory life. The plantations owned by her husband were, perhaps, less than ten miles apart. Whenever the Tories made it dangerous to be on the plantation in Chester county, she would take her children and go to the one in Fairfield.

During the year 1780 after the fall of Charleston and the march of the British through the up-country, these Tories became desperate. The houses of the Whigs were watched almost constantly and it was at the peril of his life that a Whig soldier visited his family. Mothers were forced to keep the whereabouts of their husbands a profound secret from their children. After the rout of Sumter at Fishing Creek many of the Whigs of Chester, York and Fairfield were forced to hide themselves, as best they could, and depend upon supplies carried to them by their wives during darkness of the night. Whenever a band of Tories entered a house the first thing that they asked, was, "where is the man of the house?" whatever his name was. The Whig women were plucky as the men. When they were present and the Tories would come to threaten to kill them if they did not tell where their husbands were hid, they were told that if they did kill them, Sumter would hang the last of them.

Mrs. Kilpatrick always charged her children, when she left the house, to tell anyone who might visit them during her absence inquiring for their father, that he had gone to the mill. The children knew not, but this was the fact, but the Tories understood it.

Some time during the disorganized condition of the Whig forces, Robert Kilpatrick learned that his children were all down with the smallpox. He left his hiding place and ventured to go to his house that he might look upon the faces of his little ones, perhaps for the last time. Stealthily he entered his own humble dwelling, and found his three little girls covered with the loathsome disease. In the house there was not a mouthful of bread and the only edible they had was the head of his milk cow the Tories had killed and carried off a short time before, leaving the head to the afflicted family. The heart of the strong man was filled with grief and in awful silence he sat down and rested his head upon his hands.

He had not entered the house unseen; nor was he permitted to indulge in the distressing scene which lay before his eyes. The Tories saw him when he entered, and like so many furies rushed upon him. The entreaties of his wife, the scream of his sick children were to no avail. He was seized by a band of ruffians, dragged from the house and a halter placed around his neck. What could he do? He was overpowered. A few moments and all would be over. He would not beg. Just as the awful moment approached when he was to be hanged because he was a Rebel, a horse neighed on the opposite side of the house and as all the Tories were as lazy as they were cruel, the whole band rushed out, each anxious to secure for himself the horse, Bob Kilpatrick pulled the rope from his neck and dashed for the woods, leaving both the Tories and his sick children. It was not until some time in 1781, about a year after the occurrence just related, that he dared visit his family. The Tories were made furious by his escape and swore vengeance against him if they ever put their hands upon him again. The next time that he came into the neighborhood it became known and strict watch was kept for him. By some means or other he was surprised, not in his home, but some place near Hopewell Creek. As before, the rope was fastened around his neck and all kinds of insults were heaped upon him. He was cursed and abused for making his escape on the previous occasion and told that they were determined that they would hang him this time. He seems to have come to the firm conclusion himself, that his days were soon to come to an end. The place, where he was captured, was a kind of glade and no tree being convenient it was necessary to go a few rods to find a limb upon which the unfortunate Whig might be hanged. The party was in earnest, so soon as the woods were reached they commenced the search for a suitable limb. One man with a loaded musket was left in charge of the prisoner, whilst the others scattered about some few steps from him in search for a limb.

Whilst the party was hunting for a gallows, the puppy who stood guard over him picked a piece of dry cow manure that lay nearby placing it to the nose of Kilpatrick, asked him if he did not want to smell old Ireland. This was too great an insult for Robert Kilpatrick to bear although being led to the gallows. He drew his heavy arm and with one blow laid the vile rascal senseless upon the ground and again took to the woods. The Tories shot at him, but he escaped untouched.

The Tories never put their hands upon Robert Kilpatrick again. He lived to see his country free and the names of the Tories who attempted to hang him covered with lasting disgrace. Three times he had rope around his neck to be hanged, yet he died in his own bed and we think at the advanced age of 115 years. When the war of 1812 broke out he sent two of his sons to help in driving the British from his country. A plain slab marks his last resting place in Hopewell graveyard, in Chester county, South Carolina.

Published in the *Associate Reformed Presbyterian*, journal, August 23, 1939 edition

Kirkpatrick reared several children including a daughter who married Robert Patterson. The

Gravestone of Robert Kilpatrick in Hopewell ARP Cemetery.

Patterson's daughter, Martha, married Samuel Martin Lathan.

Robert Kilpatrick lived to be 104 and is buried in Hopewell ARP Cemetery.

Section One — Grand Old Man

Samuel Martin Lathan
1797–1890

Martha Patterson
1809-1890

The son of Robert Lathan was born October 22, 1797, in Fairfield County. He was married in 1829 to Martha Patterson. He owned and farmed a plantation near White Oak, SC., on Big Wateree Creek, which flows eastward into the Catawba River.

One hundred and fifty-eight acres was purchased by him from his father in 1819 for $500.00 Later he purchased additional surrounding acreage from his brothers for a total of over 500 acres.

In 1860, he had two registered male slaves, ages 70 and 25, and listed assets of $5000 in real estate and $3956 in personal property.

During the War Between the States, Union General William T. Sherman's army passed by his plantation on their "feint" northern march from Columbia, SC.

Samuel and Martha had eleven children. He died September 1, 1890, and is buried in Hopewell ARP Cemetery in Chester County.

The eleven children included:
Reverend Robert Lathan (1829-1896) and
Samuel Boston Lathan (1842-1939)

Reverend Robert Lathan, D.D. (1829–1896)

Robert Lathan, the older brother of Samuel Boston Lathan, like his brother, sometimes called himself a "scribbler" and contributed numerous articles to newspapers and bulletins.

He was a prominent ARP minister and noted historian who graduated from Erskine College in Due West, SC, in 1855 and from Erskine Theological Seminary in 1858.

He was married in 1859 to Fannie Barron, the daughter of Dr. A. I. Barron of Yorkville, SC. He served as a Chaplain in the Confederate Army during the entire duration of the War Between the States.

Reverend Lathan lived in Yorkville for 25 years, serving as an ARP pastor, a school teacher and also county commissioner of education. He read the Old Testament from the original in Hebrew and the New Testament from Latin and Greek.

He wrote several historical sketches and is best known for his *History of the Associate Reformed Synod of the South* in 1882 and also *A History of South Carolina* (from early settlements through the Revolution) published posthumously in 2002 by this author after collecting newspaper articles in the *Yorkville Enquirer*, 1874-1876.

In addition, he published *A Historical Sketch of Union ARP Church*, Chester, SC in 1888 and *A History of Hopewell and its Pastors* in 1878. A sketch of his ancestor Robert Kilpatrick, called "*A Hero of the Revolution*," was published in 1913.

In 1881, he received the degree of Doctor of Divinity, conferred upon him at Westminster College in Pennsylvania. He was inducted posthumously into the Academic Hall of Fame at Erskine College, Due West, South Carolina, in 2002.

He taught for 10 years at Erskine Theological Seminary from 1884 to 1894, and preached in Abbeville County, South Carolina, for two years until his death in 1896.

He and his wife are buried in Rose Hill Cemetery, York, South Carolina.

Two Great Brothers

"Associate Reformed Presbyterian" March 29, 1939 Edition

In our last issue Dr. Joseph L. Grier, pastor of our Chester congregation, paid a fine tribute to Dr. S. B. Lathan, Chester's "Grand Old Man," who had recently died. Among other things he spoke of his familiarity with Latin and Greek and said that he was truly a cultured and educated man.

When we read that our minds reverted to something we had read in our files about Rev. Robert Lathan, D. D. in a sketch of the congregation of York, SC. of which Dr. Lathan was pastor for twenty-five years. The sketch was written by Mr. W. D. Grist, editor of the *Enquirer*, and appears in our files of the issue of August 11, 1920. Dr. Robert Lathan was a brother of Dr. S. B. Lathan. Mr. Grist said of him: "Dr. Lathan was probably one of the most scholarly men who ever lived in the state. He read his Old Testament from the original in Hebrew and his New Testament from the Greek and Latin, and in both cases as fluently as in English. He used his English Bible in the pulpit, but never elsewhere. He was recognized everywhere as a master of mathematics from arithmetic to calculus, and not only understood, but frequently practiced the rules by which the distance to the stars is measured.

"If Dr. Lathan had any particular hobby, it was his love for history-original research. He was especially interested in the history of South Carolina and probably dug up and wrote more South Carolina history than any one man, or half a dozen men for that matter, who ever took up the subject. He prepared a history of South Carolina from the first settlement up to the close of the Revolution, which was published in the *Yorkville Enquirer* of 1874, 1875 and 1876; but which was never published in book form because of the generally impoverished condition of the country during those days, and because the people had so much to do in keeping soul and body together they had little money with which to buy books, and not much time to read. Afterwards he completed the history of the State up to and through the reconstruction period. This was lost a few years ago in a fire that destroyed the home of his daughter, Mrs. Fannie B. Stewart."

Mr. Grist refers to Dr. Lathan's history of the Associate Reformed Presbyterian Church as his greatest and most important history. He also quotes this interesting statement which he heard Dr. Lathan make in a sermon and which he regarded characteristic of the man: "In all the years that I have been preaching, I do not know that I have ever been instrumental in bringing one single soul to the convincing knowledge of the salvation of Jesus Christ. If I were sure that I had been the means through the grace of God of converting one single soul, then I would be glad to give balance of my days to further preaching, if, for no other reason, out of gratitude to the blessed Father for having allowed to me such a blissful distinction."

Samuel Robert Lathan
1880-1942

The son of Samuel Boston Lathan was born October 10, 1880 in Chester, SC. He graduated from Chester High School in 1897, and from Erskine College in 1902. He worked for a short time with A. M. Aiken Cotton and Brokerage Company and then entered business with Frank A. Spratt. Later he formed partnership with his brother, James M. Lathan, under the firm name of the Lathan Grocery Company, which grew to be one of the most outstanding wholesale grocery concerns in upper South Carolina. Bob represented the firm as traveling salesman. After more than thirty years in business, the brothers retired in 1937.

He was a life long member of the Chester ARP Church and served on the Board of Deacons for ten years. He was a Mason, a Shriner, and a member of the Lions Club.

Caroline Mims Purvis
1899-1981

On July 15, 1929, he was married to Caroline (Callie) Mims Purvis, of Timmonsville, SC. She was a sister of Mrs. Nell Davidson of Chester and of Melvin Purvis, the famous FBI agent who captured the gangster, John Dillinger. She graduated from Columbia College where she was Vice-president of the literary society, president of the Athletic Association, captain of the basketball team, Secretary of the Student Council, member of May Court, and Editor-in-Chief of the annual.

After graduating from college, she taught in the Chester schools for many years. She was a member and past president of the Up-To-Date Book Club, Past president and charter member of the Chester Assembly, member and past president of the Violet Sunshine Club, member of the Chester County Historical Society, and a member of the Chester ARP Church.

The popular couple, Bob and Cal, took an active part in the social and civic affairs of the community in the 1930's. Their son, Samuel Robert Lathan, Jr. (the author) was born April 28, 1938.

Following a lengthy illness, Mr. Lathan died in Chester on July 3, 1942. Mrs. Lathan died October 21, 1981 in Atlanta, GA. Both are buried in Evergreen Cemetery in Chester.

Susie Meek Lathan 1879-1958

Susie Meek Lathan was born in 1879 in Chester, SC, the older sister of Samuel Robert Lathan. She lived with her father, Samuel Boston Lathan, on Saluda Street and nursed him in his later years.

The author, S. Robert Lathan, visited with his aunt frequently, spending time in the living room when he was ten years old attempting to copy the portrait of his grandfather that hung there. The portrait is now owned by a cousin, Dr. James Lathan Allen.

This Aunt Susie gave to Bob Lathan the two volumes of "South Carolina in the Revolution," by her uncle, Rev. Robert Lathan, D.D. that had been published in the *Yorkville Enquirer*. The collection of these articles on the early settlement and Revolutionary War led to the book *History of South Carolina*, published in 2002 by Bob Lathan.

Samuel Robert Lathan, Jr., M.D.
The Author

Samuel Robert Lathan, Jr., M. D. was born April 28, 1938 in Charlotte, NC. He was raised in Chester, SC and graduated from Chester High School in 1955, where he was Valedictorian and editor of the newspaper. In 1959 he graduated cum laude and Phi Beta Kappa from Davidson College where he was a member of the Kappa Alpha order and was Managing Editor of *The Davidsonian*.

He received his M.D. from the Johns Hopkins University School of Medicine in 1963 and belonged to the Pithotomy Club. His post graduate training consisted of an internship at Duke Hospital and a fellowship in Cardiopulmonary Diseases and a residency in Internal Medicine at Grady Memorial Hospital, Atlanta, Georgia.

From 1967-69 he was Chief of Professional Services at the US Air Force Hospital, Perrin AFB, Texas. Since 1969 until his retirement in 2006, he was in the private practice of internal Medicine in Atlanta. At present, he is working part – time as a consultant for the Multiple Sclerosis Center of Atlanta.

Dr. Lathan is board certified in Internal Medicine and a Fellow of the American College of Physicians and the American College of Chest Physicians. He was editor of *Atlanta Medicine* and has published numerous scientific papers. A book, *History of South Carolina* was published in 2002, as a collection of newspaper articles describing South Carolina from early settlements through the Revolutionary War. He won the Montague Award for medical writing at Piedmont Hospital in 1998 and again in 1999. He has been cochairman of the Atlanta Coalition against tobacco and served as medical director of the Main Press Center for the Atlanta Committee for the Olympic Games.

He has been chairman of four annual symposia for the Cashiers Historical Society, Cashiers, NC. A former long distance runner, he completed a total of 50 marathons and ultramarathons.

Mary Amelia Hudson Lathan

On March 19, 1966 Dr. Lathan was married in Atlanta to Mary Amelia (Millie) Hudson. Millie graduated from The Westminster Schools in 1959 as valedictorian and from Wellesley College in 1963. She earned a Masters Degree in Education from Harvard University in 1964 and later a Masters Degree in Art History from Emory University in 1990.

Millie taught at The Westminster Schools for two years and later worked for the Trust Company Bank. She was a guide for Presenting Atlanta Tours (1974-1988), and a Docent at The High Museum of Art (1975-1987). She worked for the Oxford Book Store and was Administrator of the Swan House for the Atlanta Historical Society (1989-1993). Since 1994, she has been an antiques dealer.

Her interests include folk art and pottery collecting, bridge, cooking, gardening, reading, golf, and other exercise (completing seven marathons).

The family enjoys a mountain home in Cashiers, NC and she has been very active in the Cashiers Historical Society, serving as Past Chairman of the Board. The Lathans have three children – Caroline, Stewart, and Rob, and six grandchildren.

Caroline Mims Lathan

Caroline Mims Lathan was born June 26, 1967 in Atlanta, GA. She graduated from The Westminster Schools in Atlanta in 1985 and from Brown University in 1989, magna cum laude, with Honors in Visual Arts. Caroline later attained her Masters Degree in Fine Art from Maine College of Art.

As an artist, she has won several awards including the Pollock-Krasner Award, the Creative Capital Award, the Independence Foundation Award and was a West Prize finalist. She has had numerous exhibitions in galleries and museums all over the US and Canada. Presently she is teaching art at the Upton School in Kennett Square, PA.

Caroline was married on September 25, 1993, to Van Richard Stiefel, who was born August 6, 1965 in Atlanta. Van received a BA and MA from Yale University and a PhD. in Music Composition from Princeton University. He is an accomplished classical guitarist and presently is an Associate Professor of Music Composition and Theory at West Chester University, West Chester, PA.

Caroline and Van have two children: Samuel Clark Stiefel, born February 8, 2002 in Princeton, NJ, and Charlotte Amelia Rose Stiefel, born September 24, 2005 in Montreal, Canada.

Marion Stewart Lathan

Marion Stewart Lathan was born November 8, 1969 in Atlanta, GA and graduated from The Westminster Schools where she was President of the Senior Class. In 1992 she graduated from Davidson College with a degree in Art History. At Davidson, she was Executive Board Member of Rusk House and Sweetheart of Sigma Alpha Epsilon Fraternity.

Lathan family at Millie's 70th Birthday Celebration.

After graduation Stewart worked as an event planner at the Corcoran Gallery of Art in Washington, DC. until she returned to Atlanta to work in the Creative Services Department of the Atlanta Committee for the Olympic Games. Stewart managed the design and production of specific projects including the Games uniforms, the Games medals, and the Awards Ceremonies. She was chosen as an Olympic Torch Bearer and carried it in Charlotte, NC with her father as an escort.

She has worked in school development for many years in Atlanta and London and presently is Director of Development for the Atlanta International School. A son Carrick Gray Mollenkamp, Jr. was born April 25, 2004 in Atlanta, GA.

On September 25, 2010, she was married to Robert Cameron Watkins, III in Atlanta. Robert is a graduate of Rhodes College and a tennis champion. He presently works as a software consultant and has two children: Bonnie Cameron Watkins, born January 6, 1998 and Robert Cameron Watkins IV born August 6, 2001. Together Stewart and Robert have three children.

Samuel Robert Lathan III

Samuel Robert Lathan III was born August 10, 1975, In Atlanta, GA. He graduated from The Westminster Schools in 1994 where he was Secretary of the Senior Class, an Advanced Placement Scholar, and the Discovery Outstanding Student. He played varsity football and won the Mac Shreve Award for the most improved player in 1993. He was also an outstanding varsity swimmer.

Rob graduated from the University of North Carolina, Chapel Hill, in 1998 and was a member of the Phi Delta Theta fraternity. He is presently employed in New York City in advertising and is also involved in stand-up comedy and improvisation activities. He has published a book *Get Psyched!*

He was married on May 28, 2006 to Nichol Marie Genetos, a graduate of the University of Virginia. A daughter Louise Amelia Lathan was born August 12, 2010 in New York City.

Notable Editors In The Lathan Family

Robert Lathan, Jr.

1881-1937

One of the Rev. Robert Lathan's seven children, Robert (Jr.) was born in 1881 in York, South Carolina. In 1900, he joined the editorial staff of *The State* in Columbia, SC, and served as secretary to N. G. Gonzales, founder and editor of *The State*.

In 1906, he moved to Charleston, SC, as state news editor of the Charleston *News and Courier*, and in less than four years, rose to the rank of Editor. At age 29, he was one of the youngest editors in the paper's history.

Robert Lathan, in his seventeen years as editor, remade the *News and Courier* into a twentieth-century newspaper. In 1924, he won journalism's highest award, the Pulitzer Prize, for his editorial "The Plight of the South," judged the best in the country that year.

He was President of the South Carolina Press Association in 1925-26. He was well known throughout the South and nation as an outstanding editor. He was an eloquent speaker and an active civic leader. In 1927, he moved to Asheville, North Carolina, to become editor of the *Asheville Citizen*.

Robert Lathan died suddenly of a cerebral hemorrhage at age 56 in Asheville in 1937. He and his wife Bessie Agnes Ealy are buried in Darlington, South Carolina.

In 1979 the South Carolina Press Association named him to the Press Hall of Fame.

Lapsey Barron Mills, Jr.

Born in 1927

Barron, the great grandson of Rev. Robert Lathan, was born in Mooresville, NC. and graduated from Laurinburg (NC) High School. He graduated from the University of North Carolina at Chapel Hill, receiving a degree in journalism and was elected editor of the *Daily Tar Heel*. He joined United Press worldwide news service and reported from UP bureaus in Atlanta, Memphis, Charlotte, Columbia and Raleigh before being recalled to active Navy duty during the Korean War.

After the war, he joined the *Winston-Salem Journal* and was assistant city editor, prior to purchasing the *Randolph Guide* weekly newspaper in Asheboro, NC. in 1955. He served as editor-publisher until 1991. He is the author of *Randolph County: A Brief History*.

He and his wife Barbara live in Asheboro, NC. They have three children and five grand children.

David Lathan Mims

1916-1987

David was the grandson of David Warren Lathan, the youngest of eleven children of Samuel Martin Lathan and Martha Patterson. He was born in Sumter, SC and grew up in Timmonsville, SC graduating from Wofford College in 1936. He began his newspaper career as a reporter at the *Florence (SC) Morning News*. He later became state editor of the *Spartanburg (SC) Herald*.

In WWII he began as a private in the US Army and was later promoted to the rank of Lt Col. As a journalist, he was a member of General Eisenhower's press staff, and worked on the planning staff for the Allied invasion of Normandy. He was later in charge of public relations for the Army in Belgium.

He spent a year at Harvard Law School before returning to journalism and the Associated Press in North and South Carolinas.

In 1956, he became editor of the *Daily News Record* in Harrisonburg, Virginia. During his 25 year tenure as editor, he won numerous awards.

He was president of Virginia Press Association, "Boss of the Year" 1968, "Business Person of the Year." He was campaign manager of Harry Byrd's successful US Senate race. Senator Byrd referred to him as "one of the finest persons I have ever known. His contributions to the Valley and indeed to the entire state of Virginia have been great."

A Mims Scholarship program has been established at James Madison University and Emmanuel Episcopal Church in Harrisonburg, VA.

Important dates:
1954 - Director of Development for Wofford College
1956 - Editor and General Manager of the *Daily News Record* in Harrisonburg, VA for 25 years
1962 - organized "remarch" of General Stonewall Jackson's Valley Campaign a century earlier
1981 - Retired from newspaper after winning numerous awards including best small daily newspaper in Virginia

Sandra Stovall Mims Rowe

Born in 1948

Sandy was born in Charlotte, NC and grew up in Harrisonburg, VA in the Shenandoah Valley as the daughter of Lathan Mims, the editor of the town's daily newspaper. She graduated from East Carolina University with a degree in English and married an attorney, Gerard Rowe, and began her career working for the radio station and the local newspaper. In 1938 Sandy became editor of *The Virginia-Pilot* and the *Ledger Star* in Norfolk and Virginia Beach, VA. In 1985, Lathan Mims lived to see his daughter lead the papers to a Pulitzer Prize.

After 22 years in Norfolk, she became editor of *The Oregonian*, the largest newspaper in the Northwest, and widely recognized as one of the best regional newspapers in the US. Under her leadership, *The Oregonian* won five Pulitzer prizes from 1997 to 2007.

In 2000 she was inducted into the Virginia Journalism Hall of Fame. She has been named "Editor of the Year" twice and has served as president of the American Society of Newspaper Editors.

Sandy served on the Pulitzer Prize Board from 1994-2004 and was its chairman in 2002-2003. In 2007 she retired from *The Oregonian*.

She and her husband, Gerard live in Portland OR and have two daughters.

Important Dates:
1983 - Executive Editor of *The Virginia-Pilot* and the *Ledger Star*
1985 - The paper won the Pulitzer Prize for general reporting
1993 - Editor of *The Oregonian*, the largest newspaper in the northwest
1994 - 2003 - *The Oregonian* Chairman of the Board
Under her leadership *The Oregonian* won five Pulitzer Prizes,
2008 - Editor of the Year
2000 - Virginia Journalism Hall of Fame

Lathan Family Cousins

Leila Duva Nixon Babb

Born in 1926

"Leila D" was born in Chester, SC and graduated magna cum laude in 1946 from Furman University, where she was president of the student body and listed in Who's Who.

She and her husband Lowry, a textile chemist, live in Charlotte, NC. They have five children and seven grandchildren.

George Harvey Moore

Born in 1931

George was born in Chester, SC, the great grandson of William James Lathan. He was a USAF pilot for over 20 years and retired as a Lt Col. He flew more than 500 missions over Viet Nam totaling more than 900 hours of combat airtime. He was awarded the Distinguished Flying Cross, the Purple Heart, and the Air Medal among numerous other military recognitions.

He has been President of the Chester District Genealogical Society and was instrumental in compiling and publishing *The Lathan Legacy* in 2008.

He and his wife Penny live in Chester, SC. He has three children and eight grandchildren.

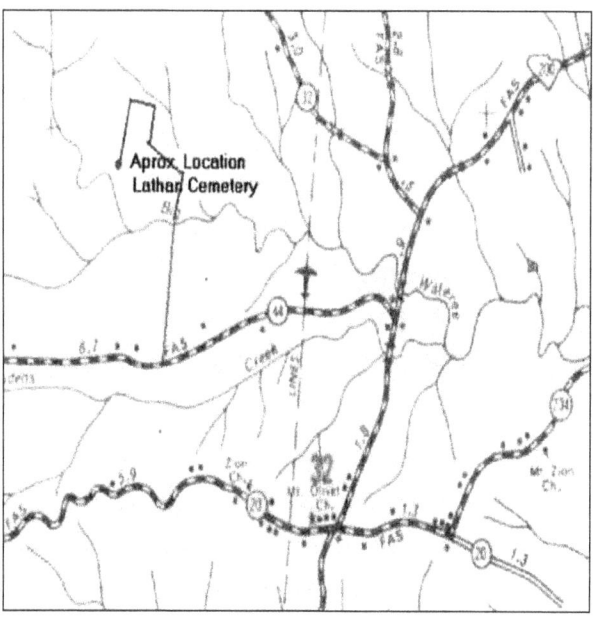

Old family cemetery near site of original Lathan plantation in Fairfield County, 2 miles East of White Oak, SC. Map provided by G. H. Moore

Robert Edward Stroud

Born in 1934

Born in Chester, SC, he graduated cum laude from Washington and Lee University in 1956. He received his law degree in 1959 from W & L University Law School where he was *Editor of The Law Review.*

Robert practiced law for over 40 years in Charlottesville, VA and taught corporate tax law at the University of Virginia.

He has two children and five grandchildren. His wife Kitty is recently deceased.

Four generations, left to right: Samuel Boston Lathan, Leila Hope Lathan, and Leila Lathan Caldwell holding Robert Stroud

Leila Caldwell Stroud Welch

Born in 1937

Leila was born in Chester, SC, the grand daughter of Leila Hope Lathan and the daughter of Leila Caldwell Stroud and Coy Stroud, the founder and first president of the Chester District Genealogical Society.

She graduated as salutatorian from her high school class in Columbus, Ohio. At Randolph Macon Woman's College she graduated Magna Cum Laude in 1959 and was Phi Beta Kappa. She was a member of Alpha Delta Pi Sorority there.

She has been very active in the Presbyterian Church, and has been especially interested in genealogy, and gardening and collecting original photography of the family. She has been an officer of the UDC and also a Regent of DAR.

In 1961 she married Houston Longino Welch, Jr., a graduate of Georgia Tech and engineer with the Southern Company for 31 years before his recent death in 2010.

In 1999 she compiled a book *My Caldwell-Lathan Family Heritage* and donated it to the Chester County Library.

She lives in Birmingham, Al has three children and eight grand children.

Augustus (Gus) Theodore Allen IV

Born in 1937

Gus was born in Columbia, SC, and grew up in Chester, SC. He attended Chester High School until he transferred to Episcopal High School in Alexandria, Virginia. After graduating from Georgia Tech he earned an MBA from Harvard Business School.

He was Vice President of Milliken Company in Spartanburg, SC for 36 years before retiring in 2000. He was inducted into the Episcopal High School Football Hall of Fame, and is on the Board of the SC Hall of Fame Selection Committee.

Gus and his wife Betty Lou live in Spartanburg, SC. They have two children and five grandchildren.

James Lathan Allen, M.D.

Born in 1939

Born in Chester, SC, he graduated in 1957 from Episcopal High School and Davidson College in 1961, where he was the author's Kappa Alpha fraternity brother. He received his MD degree from Emory University School of Medicine in 1965. He was an intern and resident in OB-GYN at the Johns Hopkins Hospital from 1965 to 1971. He was in the practice of OB-GYN in Durham, NC for 33 years before retiring in 2006.

He and his wife Julie live in Durham, NC and have two children and six grand children.

George Ashley Allen

Born in 1943

Born in Chester, SC he graduated from Episcopal High School in 1961 and from Washington and Lee University in 1965. He received a PhD in chemistry from Cornell University in 1969. At W&L he was president of Kappa Alpha Order and captain of the baseball team.

He was employed by Milliken and Company in Spartanburg for 40 years, serving as President and CEO for his last three years before retiring in 2008. In 2011 The Chemical Plant of the company in Spartanburg was named for him.

He was wife Gwin live in Spartanburg, SC and have three children and eight grand children.

Letters from Family

Mary Beth Purvis Howle, *maternal aunt of author*

Beaver Dam

DAVIDSON, NORTH CAROLINA 28036

March 30, 1988

Dear Bobby,

I checked thru Grandfather Lathan's papers with much interest. He was truly a remarkable gentleman. I used to take trips with him (before you were born) out in the County and he would tell me about the plantations and the people. I wish I had had a tape recorder (they hadn't been invented) in order to preserve the flavor that he gave the stories. There are many things I think of now that I wish very much I had asked him - but I didn't know at the time all that I needed to know.

He was a good Confederate. And in my book that makes an ancestor well worth remembering and honoring.

Since he did not go to Davidson and since we give no research degrees, there would be no place at Davidson College where these papers would be used. So I wrote to the best source for such research material - the South Caroliniana Library at the University in Columbia. I enclose the reply of Dr. Stokes and I am getting the material off to him within the next few days.

I'll be interested to know where Stewart decides to go to college.

All the best

Dr. Chalmers G. Davidson, author, historian, professor, and librarian Davidson College; distant relative of author

William L. Pressly
3770 Peachtree Road, N.E., #A-2
Atlanta, Georgia 30319

March 9, 1988

Dear Bob:

I have read all your materials with a great deal of interest. Mr. Latham was a great man. Particularly, I enjoyed the movement of his company and the battles they experienced. Of course, his account of the families and individuals around Chester fascinated me. Thomas Mackey was a fascinating character. His sentences are fabulous.

The submarines of the Civil War are wonderfully well described. It is rewarding to get such intimate information.

I am so glad I remember Mr. Latham. His sense of humor is delightful and his recall impressive.

Some one ought to select from the materials and publish the most fascinating tales.

Sincerely,
Bill

Dr. William Pressly, founder and headmaster of The Westminster Schools, Atlanta, GA, distant relative of author

Appears on a Register of

General Hospital,
Petersburg, Va.

Complaint Gunshot left thigh
Admitted
Returned to duty Jan. 5, 186 3
Deserted
Discharged from service , 186 .
Furloughed 50 days Jan. 26, 1863.
Transferred , 186
, 186
Remarks: Paroled prisoner

S. B. Latham
Co D 17 Regt S.C.

Appears on a Register of

C. S. A. General Military Hospital, No. 4,
Wilmington, N. C.

Date
Disease
Returned to duty Mch. 23, 1863
Debility
Transferred Apl. 12, 1863.
Furloughed
Discharged , 186 .
Deserted , 186 .
Died , 186 .
Post office Black

---

17 186
S. B. Latham
Co D 17 Regt S.C.

Pvt. Co

Appears on a record

Pris
at Fort McHenry, M
Date of confinement
By whom confined
Residence
How dis

(No. 40.)

SPECIAL REQUISITION.

For Private S. B. Latham Co. D. 17 Rgt. S.C.V.

One pair Shoes

I certify that the above Requisition is correct; and that the articles specified are absolutely requisite for the public service, re
the following circumstances: That I am detached on commi
and now in need of shoe clothing

S. B. Latham Co
Quartermaster,

Maj. W. G. Vaughan
By Comd Brig Genl Ripley

24 of February 186

issue the articles specified in the above requisition the 24 of February 186 in full of t
RECEIVED at Mt Pleasant One pair Shoes
Quartermaster, C. S. Army,

S B Latham
Co D 17th S.C.

(DUPLICATES.)

Section Two

Chester County's Oldest Confederate Veteran

(CONFEDERATE.)

L | 17 | S.C.

S. B. Latham
Co. D 17 Reg't S.C.

Appears on a Register of

C. S. A. General Military Hospital, No. 4,
Wilmington, N. C.

Date .... Mch 23, 1863
Disease .... Debility
Returned to duty .... Apl 12, 1863
Transferred ...., 186 .
Furloughed ...., 186 .
Discharged ...., 186 .
Deserted ...., 186 .
Died ...., 186 .
Post office Black Stock S.C.
Remarks: ....

Confed. Arch., Chap. 6, File No. 278, page 170

(635)
A. J. Douglas
3035
Copyist.

(Confederate.)

L | 17 | S.C.

S. B. Latham
Pvt., Co. D, 17 Reg't S.C.

Appears on a record of

Prisoners of War

at Fort McHenry, Md.

Date of confinement ...., 186 .
By whom confined ....
Residence ....
How disposed of Sent to Fortress Monroe Dec 29, 1862

Remarks Captured at South Mountain Sept 14, 1862

Fort McHenry, Md., Register No. 2; page 52

(639)
Copyist.

(CONFEDERATE.)

L | 17 | S.C.

S. B. Latham
Pvt. Co. D 17 Regt. S.C.

Appears on a Register of

General Hospital,
Petersburg, Va.

Complaint Gunshot left thigh
Admitted Jan. 5, 1863
Returned to duty _____, 186_
Deserted _____, 186_
Discharged from service _____, 186_
Furloughed 50 days Jan. 26, 1863
Transferred _____, 186_
Died _____, 186_
Remarks: Paroled prisoner

Confed. Arch., Chap. 6, File No. 273, page 215

W. H. Stallings
Copyist.

(635)
2249

(CONFEDERATE.)

L | 17 | S.C.

S. B. Latham
Co. D 17 Regt. S.C.

Appears on a Register of

C. S. A. General Military Hospital, No. 4,
Wilmington, N. C.

Date March 23, 1863
Disease Debility
Returned to duty April 12, 1863
Transferred _____, 186_
Furloughed _____, 186_
Discharged _____, 186_
Deserted _____, 186_
Died _____, 186_
Post office Blackstock S.C.
Remarks:

Confed. Arch., Chap. 6, File No. 278, page 170

A. J. Douglas
Copyist.

(635)
3035

Samuel Boston Lathan Timeline of War Record

March 1862	Enlisted in Company D, 17th South Carolina Volunteer Infantry at Camp Pillow, Johns Island SC
May 1862	Rantowles, SC
June 1862	Pocotaligo, SC
July 1862	Blackstock, SC home for 20 days for sick leave (jaundice)
July 1862	To Virginia – Malvern Hill – Camp Mary
August 1862	Richmond to Gordonsville to Rapidan River to Rappahanock River to Stephensburg to Orleans to White Plains to Thoroughfare Gap to Gainesville to Groveton to Hay Market to Battle of Manassas (August 30, 1862) part of Evans' Brigade at Chenin Bridge
September 1862	Chantilly to Leesburg (9/4) to Frederick (9/7) to Middleton (9/10) to Boonesboro (9/11) to Hagerstown to Funktown (9/12) to South Mountain (Battle 9/14 Wounded sent to Frederick to Baltimore
January 1863	Ft. McHenry to Ft. Monroe to City Point, Virginia in hospital two weeks to home for 30 days
March 1863	Wilmington, NC - General Military Hospital #4
April 1863	Johns Island, SC to hospital in Summervillle, SC
June 1863	Jackson, Mississippi to Vicksburg, MS (Malaria in MS)
July 1863	Vicksburg to Jackson to Brandon to Selma, AL
August 1863	Selma to Savannah, Georgia (Isle of Hope) to hospital in Columbia, SC to home in Blackstock, SC
October 1863	Mt. Pleasant, SC Commissary Department
February 1865	Left Mt. Pleasant to Strawberry Ferry to Cainhoy to Williamsburg, to Florence to Cheraw
March 1865	Averasboro, NC (Battle) to Fayetteville, NC to Bentonville (Battle March 19, 1865)
April 1865	Raleigh to Greensboro to surrender of Gen. Joe Johnston to Salisbury to Charlotte to Blackstock, SC (home)

Camps of the 17th South Carolina Regiment

In December 1861, South Carolina Governor Francis Pickens called for approximately 11,000 volunteers (10 regiments of 1100 men) to enlist for at least 12 months service due to the threat to Charleston after the Federal invasion of Port Royal in November 1861. The young men were from 18 to 25 years old. By the end of 1861, more than 27,000 men were in uniform.

Lightwood Knot Springs

Lightwood Knot Springs was a rendezvous camp for up-country troops established on the Columbia-Charlotte railroad (now the Southern RR) located south of present day Blythewood, SC near US Highway 21 about seven miles north of Columbia. It was a resort in the 1830's.

The camp was chosen by Governor Pickens in the summer of 1861 as a camp to provide instructions for the new recruits. During the war it was for one day a camp for General Sherman after he marched north after burning Columbia. During Sherman's march north his troops destroyed the railroad for 44 miles from Columbia to White Oak, SC.

Lightwood Knot Springs was later known as Camp Johnson in honor of the president of the Columbia-Charlotte railroad.

The following exerpts from letters written from Camp Lightwood Knot Springs describe some of the activities:

August 30, 1861....Here we are in camp taking our first lessons in this new kind of life. The transformation is very great, but easily borne by those who are desirous of serving their country. Our ride to Columbia presented no scenes of unusual interest; yet it is very gratifying to see the high respect paid in us by persons of all ages, sizes, colors and sexes....we reached our camp on a beautiful sandy plains....the water is good.....the health of the place is good.

August 31, 1861...Five companies leave to-day to complete Jones' regiment at Aiken (in camp Kalmia Hill)....Come down and see us, and we will give you as good as we can in our tents.

Correspondence
Carolian Spartan
September 5, 1861

Camp Hampton

Camp Hampton was located about five miles southeast of the center of Columbia on the previous Woodlands plantation of General Wade Hampton, at his old race track (now the present site of the Columbia VA Hospital). The open field served as another camp of instruction. Troops had already been assembling at his camp as early as November 1861.

Camp Lee

Camp Lee was located on the south side of the Ashley River bridge across from the City of Charleston. Many new soldiers were there issued (and used until the end of the war) old British muskets, which had been modified from the old flintlock to the newer percussion locks. The men probably were also issued uniforms at this time - gray jackets and black pants, with blue stripes up the outside seams. This was the only uniform they were ever issued. They lasted about a year. For the rest of the war the men wore what they could get.

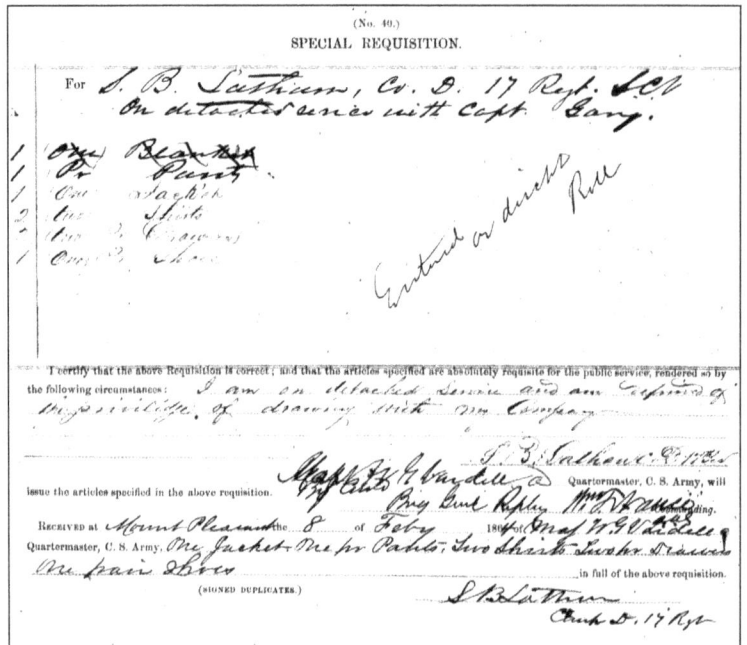

Camp Croft

Camp Croft was located on Johns Island and served as a base camp for picket duty at Rockville.

Camp Pillow

Camp Pillow was on the old Curtis Plantation with its open field very desirable for drilling troops. Curtis Hall, the plantation, was owned before and after the war by Francis Sylvester Curtis. It was located on the present day Maybank Highway near the intersection with Bohicket Road. The area's nearby boggy swamps and tidal creeks were considered "malarious" in the summer months.

Camp Simons #1

Camp Simons #1 was located at Rantowles Station on the Charleston and Savannah Railroad.

Camp Simons #2

Camp Simons #2 was located at Ravenel, 50 miles from Pocataligo.

Samuel Boston Lathan (center) at the Chester, SC War Memorial Monument

S. B. Lathan's War Record

The 17th SC Regiment of C. S. A., to which I belonged, was made up of one company from Lancaster, four from York, two from Fairfield, one from Chester, and two from Barnwell Counties. J. H. Means, former Governor of South Carolina, was the first Colonel; F. W. McMaster Lt. Colonel; and Julius Mills Major. These companies first rendezvoused near Columbia, SC in November 1861 at what was known as Lightwood Knot Springs and then were organized into a regiment at Camp Hampton with the above field officers, and after a short while were ordered to Charleston, SC or rather Johns Island nearby at Camp Pillow. Then, at this latter place I joined Company D of this regiment about the first of March 1862. We remained on the island until some time in May, when we moved camp to near Rantowles on the Savannah and Charleston railroad on account of the health of the regiment. We were engaged mostly in picket duty while on the island, and also at Rantowles. During April we had a slight engagement with the enemy's cavalry near Legare's Farm on Wadmalaw Island. Our company had two men wounded, but not seriously. This was our first time under fire of musketry.

On June the 10th, we were ordered to Pocataligo, station on the Savannah and Charleston railroad to repel in advance of the enemy from Port Royal who were endeavoring to destroy the railroad at this place and thus cut off any communication between Savannah and Charleston; but they fell back when they learned of our approach to cover their gun boats at Hilton Head and only a few shots were fired by the pickets on both sides.

Some days after our return to camp, I took the jaundice and was sent home on twenty days sick leave. While I was home the regiment was ordered on July 17th to Virginia. I rejoined them at Richmond where we camped for about a week; then we were moved down the James River near Malvern Hill.

Our brigade (commanded by General Nathan George "Shanks" Evans), composed of the 17th, 18th, 22nd, 23rd, and Holcombe Legion regiments, were for the first time all camped in close proximity to each other. (Evans' Brigade was known as the "Tramp Brigade", a reference to its ubiquity east of the Mississippi River.) We were engaged in a night attack near this place but our regiment only had a few wounded, none killed. About the first of August we broke camp and marched to Richmond, where we embarked in the cars and were carried to Gordonsville.

As soon as all our Corps (Longstreet's) arrived and were properly brigaded and provisioned with wagon trains and all the other things necessary for a marching campaign, we bid farewell to tents and I took up the line of march in the direction of Manassas to attack Pope's Army then camped near there before leaving. We were issued 3 days rations, which consisted of 1 pound of bacon, and 3 pounds of flour. The latter we prepared for cooking by working it on pieces of the heads of the barrels and cooking ash cake style, as we had no utensils. We left our knapsacks with all of your clothing except what we wore in Gordonsville. The weather was hot and dry, and after a few days marching through the dust and perspiration we did not present a very tidy appearance.

Our brigade did not get under fire of the enemy until we reached the Rappahannock River. Then we were in the most terrific cannonading I ever experienced. I should have said the evening before we would have intercepted and captured a party of the enemy's army but for a spy bringing a false order pretending to be from Gen. Longstreet to Gen. Evans, commander of our brigade, to halt and take his men back on another road, but before this spy got away he was detected, caught, and hung, all in less than five minutes. I felt sorry for him, as he begged to be shot – also gave a ring and some other mementos to an officer with a request to send to his mother (I think) in Indiana. This commotion and delay permitted the enemy to get across the bridge over the river and destroy it, and thus saved them from capture. We crossed on pontoon bridges and followed the crossing in pursuit of the enemy.

Our brigade attacked and drove the enemy back at Thoroughfare Gap – a narrow defile in the Blue Ridge Mountains. Our loss was very slight as we were halted on the farther side of the gap – a few feet from where I was. I noticed a dead Yankee and through curiosity lifted the cover (a persimmon bush) from his face. I thought he had the most pleasant and beautiful countenance I ever beheld – seemed to be about 16 or 17 years old – a smile upon his face and his light wavy hair and fair complexion made an indelible impression upon my mind. As I stood there I thought of the sadness in his home when the news would reach them their son was killed at Thoroughfare Gap.

The next day of this fight, August 29, 1861, it drizzled and rained all day. At night we camped where the woods had been cleared and the ground was strewn with brush. We soon got good fires started and were beginning to get our clothes dried when the enemy commenced shelling us, the lights of our camp making a good target. So we had to put out the fires and sleep in wet clothing. The next day we could hear the cannon of Jackson's Army engaging Pope's Army near Bull Run. We were moved by forced marches by the Dudley Ford Road and on Friday arrived at Hay Market. Everything indicated we were on the eve of a great battle. (Battle of 2nd Manassas) The next day we maneuvered all day for position. Saturday morning about 9 o'clock after lying on our arms all night we formed on the west side of the road – ate breakfast – which in our company consisted of 2 water buckets of green corn boiled with nothing but salt and water. I thought it the best "roasting ears" I ever tasted. By 11 o'clock we were in it hot and remained on the firing line until about 3 o'clock when we were relieved by McLaw's division. Our company lost 2 killed on the field, 10 or 12 wounded. The regiment lost its Colonel (John H. Means); several line officers and 27 privates were killed, and 187 were wounded. (Nearly 70% of the men in the 17th were killed or wounded). I escaped unhurt. I was one of the detail the next day to bury the dead. This we did by digging a trench about 2 feet deep and laying dead – 27 in number – in it side by side covering them with brush and earth. After we had finished these last sad rites I, with one of my company, walked over a good part of the battleground. The carnage was terrible – dead men, wounded men, Confeds and Yanks mingled together – dead and crippled artillery horses – broken cannon and small arms lay everywhere. The greatest destruction I saw was near a ravine in a little valley (not more than 2 acres) where "Wheat's Louisiana Tigers" fought the Bill Wilson's Zouaves of N. Y. and in this small space there must have been 100 dead men.

The second day after the battle the regiment took up the line of march in pursuit of the remnant of Pope's Army but he escaped to Washington D.C. We crossed the Potomac near Leesville going into Maryland on a fool's errand, as it appeared to me. There was a light frost that morning, and the water was cold. We had to wade it and continued and marched without anything of interest occurring until we halted near Fredericktown, Maryland where we remained 3 or 4 days until the baggage wagons could arrive. In the meantime, we blew up several railroad bridges in the vicinity. While here, I came near dying with an attack of cholera morbus brought on by eating too much fat back and Irish potatoes and then going to sleep on the wet ground. When we broke camp we proceeded by the pike road to Hagerstown. I managed to keep up with the regiment, but it was only the fear of capture that made me do so. We remained in camp at Hagerstown 3 or 4 days, until McClellan, who now had command of the reorganized Union forces overtook and attacked Longstreet's rear at Boonesboro or South Mountain. Our division was ordered back from Hagerstown to South Mountain - 10 miles; we left camp early Sabbath morning and arrived there in the afternoon and went directly on the firing line. After fighting for a short while, we were about to be flanked by Reno's Corps and cut off when we were ordered to fall back, which we did, and formed a new line, when we caught it heavy from all sides. I was wounded in the thigh. Two of the company were killed and 5 were wounded in about the space of 5 minutes. I should have said our company went into the fight with 16 men, almost half of whom were killed and wounded. I was left on the battlefield that night when our army fell back and remained there for 8 days. The next morning, as the Yankee army marched by where I lay, this surgeon got down off of his horse, dressed my wound, and 2 of the men carried me out to a sunny place and gave me some crackers and bacon. Also, one of them gave me a canteen full of water (I have the canteen still in my possession). **S. Robert Lathan, Jr. now has the canteen.*

Several other wounded persons were placed near me and we fared tolerably well in the way of doctors, as a great many medical students from Baltimore came up to practice on us wounded Rebs. I made out to get along in the way of eating crackers given me by the Yankee soldiers who carried me to a sunny place on the mountain. In this battle the man on my right and also on my left were both killed about the time I was wounded (I was taken prisoner).

After lying 8 days on the battlefield we were taken to Fredericktown, Maryland and placed in an improvised hospital. I remained here for about a week when some ladies of Baltimore fitted up a special hospital accommodating about 74 patients. I was one of the fortunate in getting into it. Here I remained 2 weeks when two young ladies from Baltimore made arrangements to get a Mr. Ulman of the 5th Alabama regiment and myself to go to Baltimore and spend the balance of the time out of prison on parole. This privilege was granted to the ladies by their claiming kinship with us vouching for our behavior. We remained in Baltimore about 3 ½ months during which time I had the finest time of my life - went wherever I pleased, got what ever I wanted, and it did not cost me anything. We stayed with a gentleman by the name of Pepar. He had no family, only a wife who treated us like we were children. We had a good time with the ladies attending big dinners but had to be very cautious in our talk or acts as we were liable to forfeit our parole if we did not suit the "officials" in our behavior.

When the time came for us to come across the lines we said goodbye to our "friends in need" and I shall never forget the benediction of good Mrs. Pepar as she stood with her right hand grasping mine and her left hand on my head and implored the blessing of heaven on "her dear boy" that my life might be spared through the war. We went to Fort McHenry near Baltimore and reported to the commander and requested to be sent across the lines. In a day or two we were placed on a steamer and sent to Ft. Monroe and from there to City Point near Petersburg where we were exchanged. As I was still suffering from my wound, I was sent to the hospital and remained there about 2 weeks and then I was furloughed for 60 days. I arrived home unawares to home folks as they did not know I was coming and had only heard from me once since I was captured.

About four weeks after I had returned home we had a letter from my brother William that he was in the hospital at Wilmington, NC sick with typhoid fever and wanted me to go and nurse him. This I did as soon as he was able to be furloughed home. I joined the regiment near Wilmington very soon. We were ordered to Charleston, SC and did mostly picket duty on Johns Island. On about the 20th of May 1863, we were ordered to Jackson, Mississippi. I had been sick and was sent to the hospital in Summerville, SC but never liked a hospital and got leave to join the regiment after being there only 4 days. The regiment was camped near Jackson. We remained here about 4 days when we were ordered to Vicksburg to relieve Gen. Pemberton – who was besieged by Gen. Grant in Vicksburg. We reached the Big Black River on the evening of the 3rd of July after hard marching and were getting ready to attack Grant in the rear on the next day, but before we could get out troops formed our scouts brought word that Gen. Pemberton had surrendered. This time we had to get up and get back to Jackson. On this falling back march our regiment and in fact all the troops experienced the hardest campaigning of the whole war. We marched on the 5th of July with thermometer in the nineties 20 miles along dusty roads without any water except horse ponds in the fields which I saw some drink and hardly got it down until they would throw it up again. A great many of the men fell down overcome with heat. I managed to be one of the few that made the trip but was pretty tired the next day. On the 8th the enemy appeared on our front and on the 9th we had a slight attack from them but our regiment only lost a few men. In a day or two we were ordered to fall back to Brandon, Mississippi. I was lucky in being chosen as one of the baggage guard and the baggage guard was ordered back to Selma, Alabama where we remained two weeks when the regiment was ordered from Brandon to Savannah, Georgia. The baggage guard joined later. When they passed Selma, Company D had one man killed by falling from the cars (freight box) on this trip. We were stationed at the Isle of Hope near Savannah on our arrival from Mississippi. (Whilst camped near Jackson, Mississippi, I got malaria in my system which gave me chills and although I got them broken before leaving Mississippi, I had more chills when camped at the Isle of Hope and as the local conditions there were unfavorable for breaking them up the doctor sent me to the hospital in Columbia, SC and from there I was sent home on sick leave.)

When I left Savannah for Columbia the regiment left for Charleston, SC or rather Sullivans Island. While I was at home on sick leave I received orders to report to Major W.T. Gary at the Post Commissary department at Mt. Pleasant. I had never seen Maj. Gary and do not to this day know how or why he had me detailed for duty in his office. I went to Mt. Pleasant at the expiration of my furlough and reported to Maj. Gary and found him a young man about 22 years and very clever. I remained here until the evacuation of Charleston in February of 1865. We had nice quarters and the clerical work was hard. My duty was at first to issue the bread rations i.e. meal, flour, and rice to the different commands on Sullivans Island and at Mt. Pleasant after I was employed in the office. Our pay was $11 per month.

While I was issuing clerk I had to supervise the slaughtering of the beeves. Some days we would kill as many as 50. I had about 20 men under me at work. I liked Maj. Gary very much and I know he had a good opinion of me as he frequently consulted me on particular occasions. In October of 1864 he was ordered to Virginia and Capt. H. H. Sams relieved him. I remained with Capt. Sams and had to run the whole business. He was a good man morally but had no business capacity which made it difficult for me as I had to do the business without the authority. At Mt. Pleasant there was nothing but routine work. I visited the regiment frequently on Sullivans Island. They left there in the spring of 1864 for Petersburg after which time I never saw it. I remained in the Commissary department at Mt. Pleasant.

In February of 1865 things began to look dismal. Sherman was in Savannah and was starting through SC. During the night we left Mt. Pleasant in an old wagon. Capt. Sams, Clement Sams, Jim Green, and myself and a Negro accompanying Clement Sams. This Negro left us after we had gone about a mile. The cannonading in the harbor from the enemy's guns was terrific although we were entirely out of their range. We traveled all night. About daylight we got to Strawberry Ferry on the Cooper River and after crossing it fell in with some others who were getting away from Charleston. We camped the next night near Cainhoy and the next day overtook Rhett's Brigade of regulars to which Capt. Sams was assigned as Commander. We arrived at Williamsburg and the troops then under Lt. Gen. Hardee were mobilized and the next day set out for Florence. The weather was very rainy and the roads were rough. We remained one day in Florence and took up the line of march to Cheraw while camped at night, about 9 miles from Cheraw. We were ordered to break camp and move with all possible speed as there was imminent danger of our being cut off and captured by Sherman's Cavalry.

We arrived at Cheraw early in the morning, rested all that day, and the next day loaded up all our Commissary wagons with provisions from the railroad depot and crossed the bridge over the Pee Dee River and camped just beyond. The two armies (Sherman and Hardee) engaged in an artillery fight from opposite sides of the river, after we burned the bridge. We marched leisurely each day thereafter until the advances of Sherman's Army overtook us at Averasboro - here Rhett's Brigade was on the firing line. (Col. Rhett was captured the evening before.) The next day we halted at Fayetteville and formed lines of battle, but there was only a slight skirmish between the forces. We continued falling back until we formed a junction with Gen. Joe Johnston's army which had been collected at Charlotte, N. C. and was now at Bentonville. Here Johnston gave battle to Sherman which resulted in a draw neither side gaining anything. The next day we fell back in the direction of Raleigh. When we had passed though Raleigh and were falling back to Greensboro we met some of Lee's Army when I learned for the first time that Lee had surrendered. When we were camped at Greensboro, Johnston surrendered and after preliminaries were arranged and the formal surrender was completed. We were all paid $1 in silver and drew rations from the Yankees. We marched to Salisbury, broke camp and every fellow struck out for home - in his own way - some in squads, some by two's and I managed to get to ride on the Cars to Charlotte and after remaining there one day rode to Blackstock on the train and thus forever ceased to be a warrior. I should say in the trip or march from Charleston I was not at any time required to be on the firing line being on detached duty. Yet at Bentonville I was on it at the beginning of the fight but was afterwards sent to the rear in charge of some wagons.

Samuel B. Lathan's Account of His Wounding at South Mountain and His Imprisonment at Baltimore, Maryland

On Sabbath morning the Brigade left Funktown and marched back to South Mountain arriving there about 4 o'clock in the afternoon, and were immediately deployed in line of battle on the rest of the mountain at right angles and to the west of the turnpike. On our right, the 17th SCV, had barely gotten in position when it was attacked by the 127th Pennsylvania. The fighting was terrific but we held our position until after dark when all the Confederates were withdrawn-all the severely wounded were left on the battlefield and were taken prisoner.

It was my misfortune to be among this number. I was wounded about dark and was unable to walk. I lay where I fell all night during which time I suffered the most excruciating thirst it was possible for a person to undergo. Just as we were going into battle, Col. George Jackson got my canteen to fill with water but never got it to me again as the fight was on before he returned. Early in the morning next day two Union soldiers passed by where I was lying. I asked them some water and they gave me some. Also one of them filled his canteen with water and gave it to me. I have it yet and prize it highly. I forgot the Yank's name that gave it. About 10 o'clock in the day a regiment of Yankees in line of battle passed by where I was lying and the Surgeon got off his horse, dressed my wound, and had the ambulance corps remove me a short distance near a road. He gave me a blanket and some hard tack and bacon and gave me instruction to keep the bandage on my wound moist.

I remained here until Thursday morning when, together with several wounded, I was removed to a barn about 300 yards away by the reserve ambulance Corps. We were given some rations, and those of our own wounded that could walk kept us in water. A great many of the citizens of the surrounding county visited the battlefield and would stop and look at us. They treated us somewhat similar to the way the Pharisees did the man that fell among thieves near Jericho.

On Sabbath morning September 21, just one week from the time I was wounded, I was placed in an ambulance and started for Frederick City. We stopped that night at Middletown, and I slept in the ambulance in the streets. The next morning the lady of the house near where the ambulance was standing sent a servant to inquire if I would like to have a cup of coffee. I told her yes and a regular breakfast. She sent out a good breakfast for two, as there was another wounded boy in the ambulance with me. He would not eat any of it. I drank both cups of coffee and wrapped up his portion and put it in my havensack for future use. But we had scarcely gotten out of town before he begged me out of it, saying he would not take it from a Yankee, but would from me. I failed to see the difference.

We arrived at Frederick City about 12 o'clock and were placed in an old tanyard building improvised as a hospital. There was a large crowd of ladies from Baltimore there, and they were profuse in their act of kindness, furnishing us with nice clothing and all the delicacies both to eat and drink. I was beset by about a dozen of these ladies wanting the brass buttons off my uniform. I gave them my coat to get the buttons. I have never seen coat or buttons since. However, I got a nice suit in place of it. After remaining here four days, I had the good fortune to be removed to a special hospital fitted up by the ladies of Baltimore capable of accommodating 15 patients. Here I fared royally.

After remaining here 10 days, two ladies from Baltimore persuaded me to go to Baltimore with them, promising to get me a nice place to stay in a private home. They made all the arrangements with the Surgeon in charge of the hospital and also with the Commandant of the post for my parole. The ambulance was to be at the hospital to take me to the depot in time for me to get on the train. But lo! When the ambulance drove up, the hospital steward refused to let me go. The ladies after waiting at the RR station to nearly the last minute for the ambulance, came to the hospital to see what was the matter, blessed out the steward, and placed me in the ambulance and got in themselves. We hurried to the station, but the train was gone.

They paid the driver to take us to the Monacy Junction 4 miles away to endeavor to catch the train on the B & O RR, but got there too late. We went to a farmhouse and put up with the proprietor until the next evening. I think the gentleman of the house was favorably inclined to the Confederacy and did not want it known that I was a Confederate prisoner for he might get into trouble. The next evening (Sabbath) we left. Out host got to the station in ample time for the train. A regiment of troops was camped in the station. I don't think I ever heard as much profanity used in some time as I did by these soldiers.

While sitting at the station, I could see the grounds we had camped on only a few days before. Then the stores were all closed and the county looked deserted. Now it was all life. Two Yankee soldiers carried me in the train (I could not walk much), and I got a seat next to my two lady friends. I suffered a great deal from my wound, owing to being forced to keep my limb in a cramped-up position. I was also annoyed by some passengers wanting to know if I was sick and if so, what was the matter. This, however, was soon brought to a quietus by one of the ladies telling a very inquisitive person that she was afraid her cousin (as that was what they called me) was taking small pox.

I arrived at Baltimore about 9 o'clock (Sabbath night) and drove directly to the residence of Charles H. Pepar (814 West Baltimore St.) who was waiting our arrival. I was taken to my room after a short while.

Sources:
Soldiers Record, S.B. Lathan, National Archives, Washington, D.C.
Proceedings of Southern Historical Society; Prince William County Public Library, Bull Run Branch, Manassas, Virginia
Family Records held by George Moore of Chester, SC and William C. Lathan, Jr. of Triangle, Virginia

Battle of South Mountain Boonsboro, Maryland September 14, 1862

Following the success of the Battle of Second Manassas, Virginia, also known as the Battle of Bull Run, Confederate General Robert E. Lee sought to take the war to northern soil. Lee proposed a bold plan to lead his Army of Northern Virginia to strike simultaneously into western Maryland to seize the Federal arsenal at Harper's Ferry, West Virginia and to invade Maryland.

Realizing that the Confederate Army was split, the Army of the Potomac under Major General George B. McClellan pursued the Confederates to Frederick, Maryland and then advanced on South Mountain, a continuation of the Blue Ridge Mountains in Maryland. On September 14, 1862 pitched battles were fought for possession of the three South Mountain passes: Turner's, Fox's, and Crampton's Gap. Confederate Major General D. H. Hill, deploying 5000 men over more than two miles, defended both Turner's Gap and Fox's Gap.

The night before, General Lee had ordered General James Longstreet's command, consisting of Major General David R. Jones and Brigadier General Nathan G. Evans divisions to march from Hagerstown Maryland to Boonsboro on the 14th. Longstreet did not start his march until mid-morning. Along the way, he received a report from Hill that he was under attack and needed reinforcements badly. Longstreet's troops immediately increased their pace along the 20 mile route. With the road very dusty and hot, several stragglers were left behind.

Meanwhile at Turner's Gap, Gen. Hill ascended a lookout station near an old tavern alongside the National Road (or Pike) called the Mountain House. A spectacularly beautiful view of the Middletown Valley spread out before him. However the view that morning was disturbing as thousands of Union troops were storming up the mountain along the National Pike.

General Joseph Hooker, who commanded his First Corps on the right flank, had sent for General George Meade's Third Division also known as the Pennsylvania Reserves, to ascend and attack Hill's left flank. The terrain was described as "rough, rugged, and steep". Colonel Albert Magilton commanded his brigade consisting of the 4th 7th and 8th Pennsylvania Reserves.

Around 4 pm, Gen. Hill had sent General Robert Rodes with his five Alabama regiments to the Frosttown Road Gorge. Col. Peter F. Stevens reported at the head of Gen. Nathan Evans brigade followed soon after by Gen. John B. Hood's division. Hill ordered Stevens to report to Rodes north of the National Pike. When Longstreet arrived later, he sent Hood south to Fox's Gap.

Col. Stevens had 550 men in his SC Brigade with five regiments (17th, 18th, 22nd, and 23rd SC and the Holcombe Legion). The 17th SC formed south of the Dahlgreen Road. Magilton's Pennsylvania Reserves overwhelmed Col. Steven's South Carolinians. Of the 550 men, in less than one hour, 23 were killed, 148 wounded, and 45 captured. The 17th SC lost 61 of its 149 soldiers, among them Maj. Stark Means (Col. John R. Means brother) and Col. Fritz McMaster sustained a severe thigh wound.

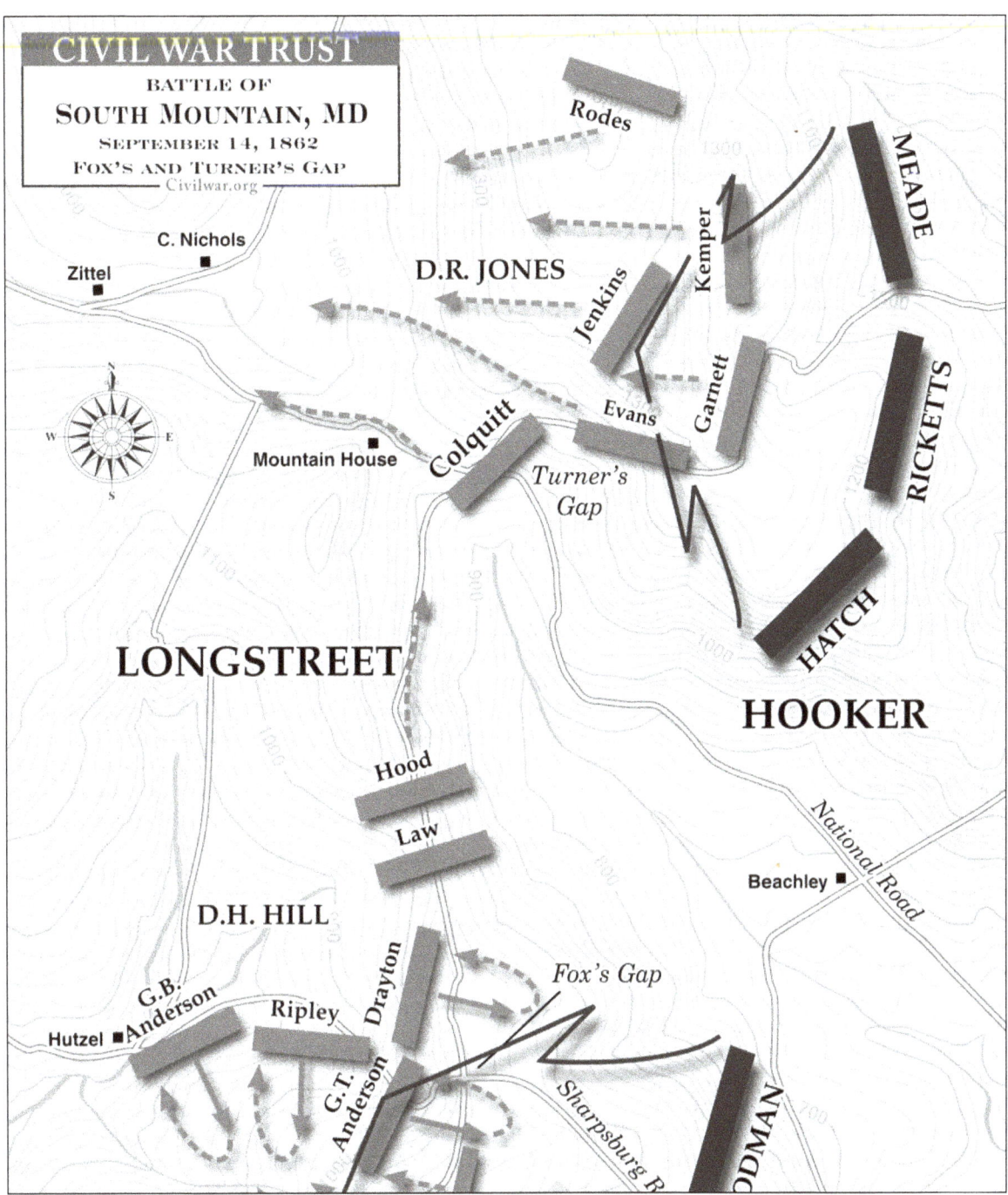

At nightfall (around 6pm) the Confederates still held the Gap despite being outnumbered 2 to 1. Lee's Army delayed McClellan's advance for a day before withdrawing.

Two days later, the Battle of Antietam, sometimes called the Battle of Sharpsburg, on September 17, 1862 would become the bloodiest battle of the war. Lee was at that point forced to abandon his invasion of Maryland.

D. Rent House was in the direct line of battle of the Pennsylvania Reserves and the 17th SC Regiment

Maryland Historical Trust
State Historic Sites
Survey F_4_120
D. Rent House
1741 Dahlgren Road
Middletown, MD

This property is included in the survey of resources associated with the Civil War Battle of South Mountain, which occurred On September 14, 1862. The Daniel Rent House is situated in a sharp bend of Dahlgren Road just north of Turner's hill. Probably built in the mid 19th century, of log construction, the house was later enlarged as indicated by a break in roof lines and in window pattern. .... The eastern elevation of the house afforded a clear view of the advance of General Hatch's Division of General Hooker's I Corps, as they made their way toward Turner's Gap which was held by Confederates under Generals D. H. Hill and James Longstreet.

US Army Corps of Engineers maps from the Civil War show the D. Rent house in the direct center of Hatch's line of advance.

The fight to control Fox's and Turner's Gaps was bitter resulting in many casualties on both sides.

The Rent House, on the Frosttown (now Dahlgreen) Road, south of the "Mountain House", dates back to 1840.

Backyard of the Rent House: the estimated site of Samuel Boston Lathan's wounding by the Pennsylvania Reserve

Runner to pass where Confederate grandfather was wounded

Chester native enters ultramarathon

By Glinda Price, Lifestyle Editor
News and Reporter, Chester, SC
Wednesday, November 19, 1986

"On the first day's fighting (September 14, 1862) of the battle of Sharpsburg, MD. I was wounded severely and left on the battlefield, where I remained a week, " wrote Samuel B. Lathan of Chester in the *Chester Reporter* on December 22, 1938. He was recalling his experience during the War Between the States.

This Saturday, Nov. 22, his grandson, Dr. Robert (Bob) Lathan of Atlanta, a Chester native, will be very near the site where his grandfather was wounded and lay on the battlefield. He will be running in an ultramaraton, the John F. Kennedy 50 mile hike-run, and the race has special meaning for that reason.

"I heard about this race 10 years ago," Dr. Lathan said by telephone from his Atlanta medical office. "I really wanted to do it, because it was different and I had an interest in that section of the state where the ultramarathon was taking place."

In the battle of South Mountain, a smaller battle before the actual battle of Antietam on Sept 17, 1862, Lathan was wounded in the thigh. He was left on the battlefield and, a week later, was taken prisoner to Frederick, MD.

Author on South Mountain during JFK 50

He was the last veteran of that war ....in Chester and he died in March 1939 at the age of 96.

Dr. Bob Lathan has recently been researching his grandfather's life and is looking forward to his run past the place where he, along with many other Confederates, was wounded. It was a battle that was considered the bloodiest of the war.

"I have visited the Antietam Battlefield," Dr. Lathan said. "There is some beautiful country up there."

This ultramarathon has an interesting history. An ultramarathon differs from a marathon in that it is 50 miles as compared to 26 miles. The JFK 50 mile Hike-Run was begun in 1963 after the death of President Kennedy.

"The JFK 50 is the oldest ultramarathon in the U.S.," Lathan said.

The ultramarathon got its start when President Kennedy, in the early 1960's came across an executive order dated 1910 and signed by President Theodore Roosevelt that said every Marine should be able to run or hike 50 miles in 20 hours. This amazed Kennedy and he asked Marine officers if anybody could do this.

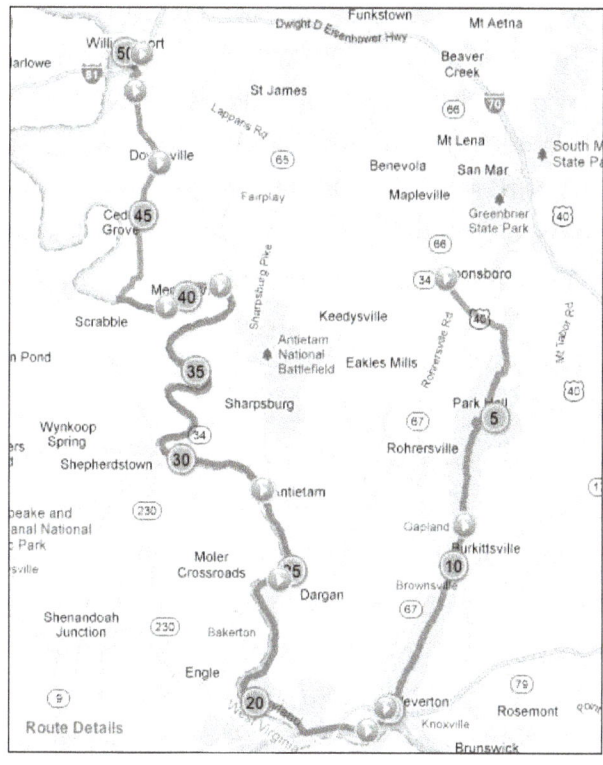

JFK 50 Route

One of these officers was Buzz Sawyer, the founder of the JFK 50, who got some of the Marines interested in doing just that. At Kennedy's death, the ultramarathon was formed as a commemorative race.

The race, which is actually 50.2 miles, begins in a small town in Maryland, Boonsboro, and ends in Williamsport, MD............follows about 15 miles of the Appalachian Trail and passes through many sections that are rich in Civil War history: Harper's Ferry, near Antietam; Shepherdstown, W. VA, and is near the South Mountain Battlefield.

"There is a point up there, at Harper's Ferry, that is absolutely beautiful," Lathan said. "That's where the Potomac and Shenandoah Rivers join."

Lathan says that it should take him 10 to 12 hours to finish the race that has an allotted time of 14 hours. He wanted to run the race several years ago but some health problems prevented his participation.

"I'm not quite at the endurance point where I was," Lathan said, "but I'm not worried about the time. I just want to finish it."

Lathan has been training for about four months, running about 40 miles a week. His training program includes a lot of stretching exercises also.

He has run many marathons in various parts of the country, but only two other ultramarathons.

Dr. Lathan's grandfather was a well known man of Chester. He was born near Blackstock and, as a young man, hoped to study law, but his plans were interrupted by the war. Following the War Between the States, he taught school for a short time but later was a bookkeeper and cotton factor in Chester.

He was a great believer in learning and was given a Doctor of Literature degree from Erskine College in 1934 for his scholarly attainments.

Dr. Samuel Lathan was proud of being a Civil War veteran and he probably would be just proud of his grandson's achievements.

Sherman's Carolina Campaign and Feint Tour

When Union Major General William T. Sherman and his 63,000 troops entered South Carolina in January-February 1865 after capturing Savannah, there was virtually no resistance. Sherman's men took their revenge at every farm, plantation and town from Savannah to Columbia.

Sherman marched his armies in multiple directions simultaneously, confusing the scattered Confederate defenders as to his first true objective: the state capitol of Columbia.

On February 17th Columbia surrendered to Sherman and many soldiers took advantage of ample supplies of liquor in the city. Fires began and high winds spread the flames across a wide area, destroying most of the central city. After burning Columbia, Sherman's next objective was either Raleigh or Goldsboro in northern North Carolina. However to keep the Confederates guessing, he decided to "feint" directly north of Columbia in the direction of Charlotte, NC. Sherman's "bummers" were foragers who operated in front of the main regiments and destroyed the railroads along the way. General Grant had asked Sherman, "What's to prevent their laying the rails again". Sherman smirked and replied, "Why my bummers don't do things by halves. Every rail having been placed over a hot fire has been twisted as crooked as a ram's horn and they are never to be used again."

After burning Winnsboro, SC on February 21st, Sherman headed north toward White Oak, SC and Blackstock, SC. In front of the nearby Hopewell Reformed Presbyterian Church, there is a monu-

General Sherman's "Bummers" methodically take apart the tracks of the Charleston and Savannah Railroad. Harper's Weekly, *courtesy of Thomas Fetters (Harpers Weekly).*

ment to a black slave, Burrell Hemphill who was "killed by Union soldiers February 1865."

Sherman's men then turned northeast toward Cheraw, SC and Fayetteville, NC, and a few miles east of White Oak, SC, passed by the plantation of Samuel Martin Lathan on Big Wateree Creek, which flowed eastward into the Catawba River. Then to end the feint, they linked up with the rest of Sherman's Army.

Meanwhile, part of Sherman's forces had left Savannah toward Charleston, destroying the entire Charleston and Savannah railroad. On February 11th, General Beauregard had ordered General Hardee to evacuate Charleston immediately and march northwest to Chester, SC as an assembly point. Hardee delayed evacuation until the 18th and then had to change plans and moved toward Cheraw instead of Chester.

Section Two — Chester County's Oldest Confederate Veteran

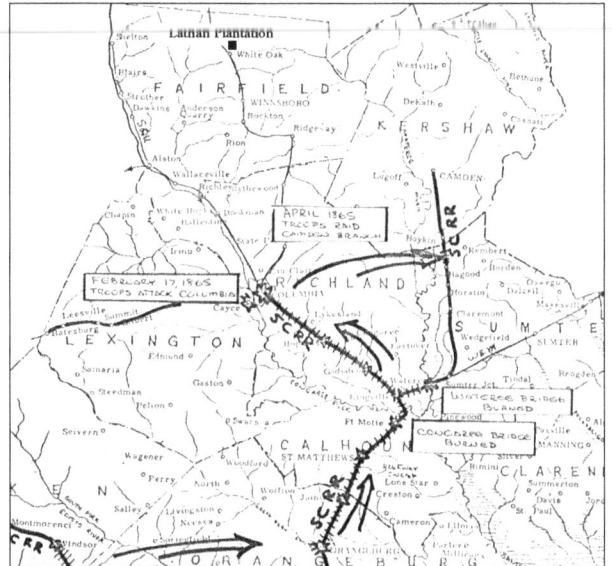

Sherman's troop movements across the State of South Carolina including the Lathan Plantation. Courtesy of Thomas Fetters (Harpers Weekly).

Sherman's Burning of Samuel Martin Lathan's Plantation

The Chester Reporter
Samuel Boston Lathan's interview at age 96
October 13, 1938

When he [Samuel Boston Lathan] came home from the war, he discovered that Sherman's army had passed through his father's plantation on his march through South Carolina.

He saw no living thing as he came in sight of his home, not even the dog with his usual welcome. His father met him and told of the devastation Sherman and his soldiers wrought upon their farm.

When word came that the army was coming, the elder Mr. Lathan hurriedly filled their 2-horse wagon with corn and piled fodder on top, thinking the soldiers wouldn't bother a wagon seemingly filled with fodder. This he pulled away to the field. He hid a side of bacon and a sack of flour in a closet under the stairs and turned out all the animals.

When Sherman's soldiers arrived, they collected all the live stock except one small mule and five sheep that had wandered too far away. They slept on the cotton and burned it after their night's rest, and also burned the wagon with the fodder. The soldiers poured out all the sorghum that they couldn't eat and destroyed everything in sight. When marching away one of the soldiers attacked by the dog barking at them, raised his Yankee rifle and shot the innocent dog.

Mount Pleasant, South Carolina Commissary, 1865

Suzannah Smith Miles, a historian in Charleston, SC provided the research concerning the location of the Confederate Commissary on Mount Pleasant (now on Pitt Street). It was placed in the general store of Henry Slade Tew, who was the indendant (mayor) of Mount Pleasant during this period. Also Lucas Mill at Shem Creek was used.

The following letters that Tew wrote to his daughter were copied by Mrs. Miles from the originals in the Charleston Library Society.

The Federal troops had occupied the coast around Charleston since 1862 until they took possession of Mount Pleasant in early March, 1865. The Confederate Army Muster Roll shows that Samuel Boston Lathan was "temporarily detached from 17th Reg. detailed in Commissary Dept."

> (Confederate.)
>
> S B Lathan
> Pvt — 17 Regt S.C.
>
> Appears on a
>
> **Muster Roll**
>
> of Officers and Men paroled in accordance with the terms of a Military Convention entered into on the 26th day of April, 1865, between General Joseph E. Johnston, Commanding Confederate Army, and Major General W. T. Sherman, Commanding United States Army in North Carolina.
>
> Roll dated _Not Dated_
> _____, 1865.
> Paroled at _Greensboro North Carolina_, 1865.
>
> Enlisted:
> When _____, 186_.
> Where _From Fairfield SC_
> By whom _____
> Period _3 yrs_
>
> Last paid:
> By whom _____
> To what time _____, 186_.
>
> Present or absent _Present_
> Remarks: _Temporarily detached from 17 SC Regt. detailed in Commissary Dept._
>
> Number of roll:
> 498
> (639e) A M Crosby / Copyist.

February and March 1865
Henry Slade Tew
Letters

On Thursday, the 16th Feby about three o'clock the military began to impress all the Carts, Wagons, Horses and Mules in the Town, and then at length all were convinced that the time was come. About 10 o'clock that night Mr. Porcher (13) came to my house, having ridden near 40 miles, to request me to dispose of the corn on his plantation (about 300 bushels) to the people in such quantities as they needed and to give such as had no means of purchasing. And, on Friday morning, Dr. Bonneau (14) who was about removing his family, made the same request as to Rough Rice (about 400 bushels), but the absence of all the Carts prevented me from carrying out their requests. Directly after breakfast I heard that the commissary was going to sell at the mill all the stores he could not remove. I went up and succeeded in purchasing some flour and meal for myself, and also in getting a few sacks of each for the poor, which I paid for myself. I had previously collected some Rough Rice and corn for the Poor, which I had at the mill and in my store, and had made distribution of about 80 bushels to some of the families.

.....that day Friday (February 17) was one of anxiety to us all. About dark all the batteries on Morris Island and some of the vessels commenced the most terrible fire I think I ever witnessed in the war, directed at Sullivan's Island principally, though Sumter came in for a share, with the view to cut the bridge (16) and prevent evacuation of the Island. The fire was incessant and seemed to extend up to our bridge. It was a grand but awful scene. Mrs. Caldwell (17) sent to ask me if I thought she was in danger, and we advised her to come to our house, which she did with her family. The awfulness of that night must dwell in the

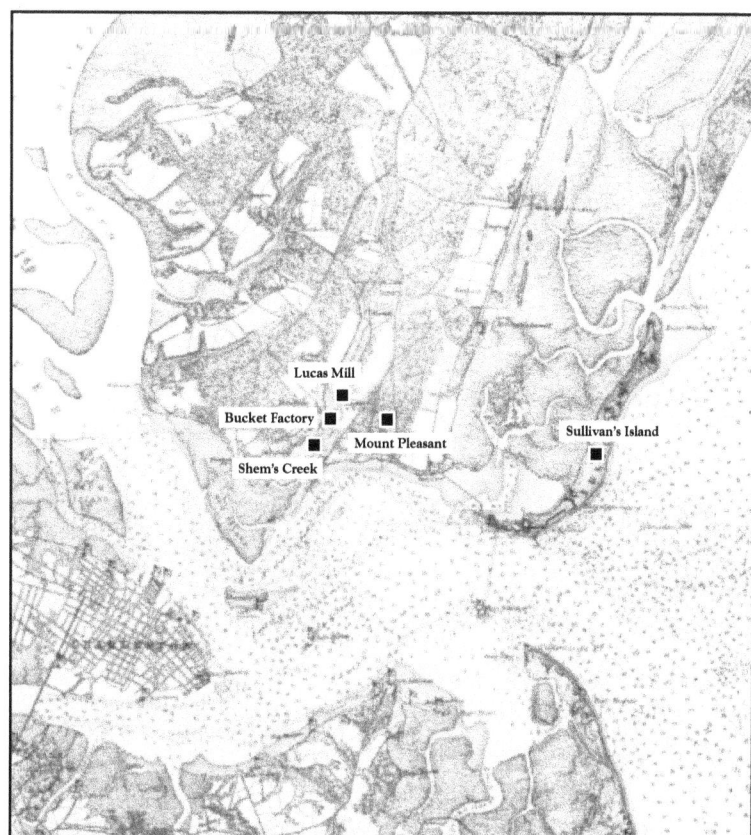

The Commissary in Mt Pleasant served the region of Charleston

minds of those who witnessed it as long as memory lasts. In the midst of it, I received a message from Major Vardell (18) to come to his quarters, and went immediately. I found him and his clerks, Tomlinson and Hall (19) ready to move, and he told me that he had left a quantity of corn in the store at the mill which he wished me to dispose of to the people as early as possible next day at Government price of $5.00 per bushel. He wished the distribution as general as possible, at the same time I heard that orders had been given to burn the mill and contents, and about 1200 bushels of Rough Rice of which near 200 was my own, and I had also the stores for the poor in it.

I regarded this as a wanton act of cruelty, as ours was an isolated community having no local source of supply, and all that was in the mill would not have afforded more than would suffice to feed them a month or two, and the destruction of the mill itself would deprive the people of a means of having any rice beat or corn ground, and must cause great suffering. I therefore determined to be there before daylight and endeavor to prevent destruction. Accordingly I rose before day and went there. Just as the sun was rising a squad from Bolton's Calvary (20) rode up with torches. I remonstrated with the officer representing the importance of the mill to the people, but in vain, the order was imperative and at the moment Capt. Bolton himself came up, and to him I also appealed: He admitted cruelty of the act, knew from his long service at this post that the mill was the only source for the inhabitants to prepare their grain for food, but his orders compelled him to destroy it, and fire was accordingly applied, and the devilish act, I must call it, accomplished.

Before the destruction was completed, I succeeded in getting the mill opened and as my own rice was in sacks, I had it thrown out and distributed to the crowd without distinction of person or color. I then disposed of the corn in the same manner to white and black trying to make the distribution as nearly equal as I could. Many of them paid but some too needy I gave it to...much no doubt was stolen, as we have had a lawless population for some time in our town.

While these scenes were transpiring over here, those of Charleston must have beggared description—to us was visible only the awful magnificence of the scene, while the terror, confusion, suffering and crime must have been appalling to the dwellers in the doomed city. The burning buildings, public and private, the repeated explosions, the gun boats and other vessels burning in the harbor all presented such a scene as but few every witness in a lifetime, an surely one which none would ever desire to see repeated. Oh God! What a night of horror that memorable 17th of February was.

...Monday 20th we heard that the troops that had landed at Bull's Bay were marching down and about 11 o'clock the shouts of the black people apprised us of their arrival. There were three regiments of U S black troops all under the command of Col. A. S. Hartwell who took his quarters temporarily at the light house. I called on him, told him my name and position and asked protection for the persons and property of the citizens who were mostly women and children and were greatly apprehensive a the presence of the black troops. He received me very courteously, and assured that the fears of the people would prove unfounded as the troops were under better restraint than we imagined and directly placed them in camp and gave stringent orders against straggling from camp and forbidding them to enter houses or otherwise molest citizens. Colonel Hartwell then entered into conversation with me, asked if I was connected with the Tews of Rhode Island and if I was favorable to secession, as he had received so many assurances from people that they were not, that he was at a loss what to think and could only judge by the manner and not the language. I told him I would reply with the utmost frankness, that if more than one man in South Carolina out of Fifty told him he had opposed secession they lied, and that for myself, a Union man in 1832 and in 1850, yet on the election of Mr. Lincoln I thought all hope of justice to the South in the union was lost, and I went for secession with vote and voice. He thanked me for the frankness of my reply and said it would be better if all would be equally so. Soon after I left he called on me at home, and I put him in Mr. Whilden's house as "headquarters" by which means Mr. W's furniture has been saved to him as some of the Rogues had broken into the house on Saturday night and stolen. I named the suspected party and on intimation from the Col., the fellow brought it all back the same day.

February

The excitement .....was intense. Many of the blacks from the Plantations came down in the Army train, and together with those of the village made quite a multitude of shouting wild creatures whom the thought of freedom had changed from quiet to transports of uproarious joy. I must tell you what I did for my own. A few days before I gave them $50.00 told them the money would soon be worth nothing and advised them to buy whatever they could then. I also told them that when the troops came they knew they were free to go or stay as they pleased - if they stayed, as long I had anything to eat they should share as they always had done. Not one answered a word, and I knew of course they would go – they stayed however until Wednesday, and then went off without a word of leave taking – Sary setting the example – Louis is gone also, Margaret and Zoe are still here as Elisa is with William and forbids their leaving, but I suppose they will not stay long....

....two or three squads of soldiers started into the premises on Monday before guards were placed seeking for tobacco, and stole from me a spy glass...some trifling articles – the night of Monday passed quietly and we began to hope that under the firm hand and rule of Major Nott the Prov. Mar. things would soon be bearable. When orders came from the Brig. to move to the city and they left us with only six men as guard and our Blacks noisy, stealing all they could lay hands on and moving into the houses that were vacant. It was sleepless night to us. We all sat up till 4 o'clock. Wednesday was a quiet day. Wednesday night we went to bed very early, no troops yet came over, and we left a light burning. About midnight a ring at the bell and an order to open the house. I put on some clothes and admitted soldiers, white, who said they came from Sul. Isd. And seeing a light in only my house desired to examine. They asked a number of questions, seemed satisfied with the replies and left. Not long after I heard a clash of arms and a request for some fire. I handed them some matches and all was quiet the rest of the night. Since that night, order is fast being restored, the blacks not allowed to enter houses or commit depredations, and I must say that every officer with whom that I have had intercourse has exhibited a degree of courtesy and I must say kindness of manner to me most unexpected from all that we have heard of the conduct elsewhere and the threats against So Ca particularly. I have had intercourse with Gen.

Potter, Col. Hartwell, Lt. Col. Fox, Major Nott, Capts. Taylor, Sharp and Abeels, and Lieuts. Pollock & Anderson, besides meeting many Naval and Military on the streets, and I have never either by word or look have been made to feel that I encountered a foe. I have had no conversation with anyone but Col. Hartwell as before related. Capt. Abeels is our Prov. Mar. but his Regt. Was about to be withdrawn and the 53rd Pennsylvania to come... Out ladies have borne up bravely and have behaved with much prudence.

March 1, 1865

The 52nd Regt. Major Hennessy, Com'g now garrison Mount Pleasant. Headquarters are now established at Mr. Whilden's house and the proximity to our dwelling is the best guaranty we can have of quiet and order. The commander seems to be determined to enforce order and maintain stricter military discipline than we have ever had over here before from the troops of either army. He does not appear to have much sympathy or regard for blacks, at least he does not place them above the whites and make all claims and interest subservient to theirs. He called on me and was social and pleasant....

March 7, 1865

...On the 7th they took possession of my store and placed their Sutter in it, but by arrangement with him, I am to be paid rent. The Sutter, Dr. Lowie is a Scotchman, and seems desirous to settle in business here, and I may possibly find employment from him, at any rate the rent of the store will give me the means of meeting the taxes that will probably be imposed and relieve my mind of much apprehension on that score....

General Nathan G. "Shanks" Evans (1824–1868)

"Shanks" was born in Marion, SC, in 1824. Evans graduated from Randolph Macon College at the age of 17 before entering West Point with the endorsement of John C. Calhoun. At the "Point" he graduated at the bottom of his class in 1848. However, he established himself as a fighter on the frontier against the Indians and in the Mexican War.

He was a Confederate Colonel at the Battle of First Manassas but was sad after his good friend and former best man, Gen. Barnard Bee, was killed. Evans was promoted to Brigadier General in October, 1861. His brigade was so well traveled—fighting in so many battles—it was nicknamed the "Tramp Brigade" and was one of the South's most famous units.

In the summer of 1862 at Second Manassas (one of Lee's greatest victories), Evans' Brigade lost hundreds of men in heavy fighting, including Col. John Means of the 17th SC regiment.

Despite his battlefield success, Evans was somewhat controversial and was subject to two courts-martial in 1863. In both trials he was acquitted of the charges, but his reputation was ruined. He had conflicts with Gen. John B. Hood and especially with Col. Fitzhugh McMaster.

He died in 1868, most likely from the residual effect of his previous severe head injury in 1864, when his head struck the cobblestones as he fell from a buggy on Meeting Street in Charleston.

General Joe Johnston in North Carolina

Despite his serious misgivings, President Jefferson Davis restored Gen. Joseph Johnston to active duty on February 25, 1865. Johnston assumed command of the Department of North Carolina and Southern Virginia on March 6. His command consisted of approximately 20,000 men including 12,000 under Gen William J. Hardee.

Gen. Hardee delayed Gen. Sherman at the Battle of Averasboro on March 16. The last major battle of the Carolina Campaign, at Bentonville, from March 19-21, involved approximately 80,000 men - 60,000 Union troops and 20,000 Confederate troops. At Bentonville, General Johnston displayed unusual boldness and the Confederate troops fought valiantly despite being severely outnumbered. Sherman allowed Johnston to escape to Smithfield, NC toward Raleigh, while he traveled to Goldsboro for supplies.

In early April 1865, Johnston received dispatches on Lee's activities in Virginia, and when Richmond fell, Sherman planned to move on Johnston, who then proceeded toward Raleigh and then to Hillsboro, NC. On April 11, Johnston learned of Lee's surrender of April 9, and left his troops under the command of General Hardee and reported to Jefferson Davis who was escaping from Richmond near Greensboro, NC on April 12.

Johnston saw the futility of further resistance, and suggested a meeting with Gen Sherman between Hillsboro and Durham, NC. A small farm house, Bennett Place was chosen and after three separate days of negotiations (April 17, 18, and 26,) Johnston surrendered to Sherman, 2 ½ weeks after Lee's surrender at Appomattox, essentially ending the Civil War. Sherman initially suggested that the Confederate Armies disband and that there would be a general amnesty. His proposal actually guaranteed the right of property of slaves.

In Washington, Secretary of War, Edward Stanton was frantic at Sherman and rejected Sherman's terms of surrender. Stanton ordered Grant to go south and meet with Sherman. Grant arrived in Raleigh on April 24 and ordered Sherman to reopen negotiations. General Sherman and Johnston met again in the Bennett House on April 26 and agreed that the Confederate Army was to disband and leave its munitions in Greensboro and not to resist.

Samuel Boston Lathan

Section Three

Profound Source of Information

Mr. S. B. Lathan Had Quest For Learning

The Chester Reporter
By W. J. Irwin, April 8, 1959

Samuel B. Lathan, author of the article, which I have been reviewing, was born at the family homestead east of Blackstock, May 2, 1842. His formal education was limited to the years he attended the Blackstock school under the tutelage of Matthew C. Elder, who was considered a most capable teacher. The school term in the "old field" schools of that day was in all probability not longer than five or six months as compared with the nine months session of today. Mr. Lathan was most likely an omnivorous reader who retained most of what he read.

As the years progressed young Lathan had virtually determined to study law. Then the War Between the States broke out and his plans, like those of so many other promising young men, were rudely shattered. When after four years he returned from the war he was a grown man with conditions entirely different, and it was too late to take up his plans afresh, but rather to retrieve what he could from the wreckage and start anew. Laboring first as a teacher, then as a book keeper, then as a cotton factor, he never let up in his quest for learning, but utilized every opportunity to increase his stock of information. It is impossible in any other way to account for his vast store of knowledge—his proficiency, particularly in Latin, Greek, history, philosophy, and mathematics. He was equally as well versed in the Bible and religious subjects generally, and probably more so. As a token of its deep appreciation of his wide range of learning and his scholarly attainments Erskine College in 1934 conferred upon Mr. Lathan the degree of Doctor of Literature. No honor of the kind was ever more worthily bestowed.

I can imagine that even on the battlefield at the end of a hard day's fighting, with enemy, perhaps, only a short distance off and likely to attack at any moment, Mr. Lathan would get out what books he had available and pore over them by the campfire's flickering light. It was by taking advantage of every opportunity to learn that he acquired his marvelous stock of information.

During Mr. Lathan's leisure time he had frequently tutored boys and girls who were preparing for scholarships or entrance examinations. Very rarely, if ever, did any of his pupils fail to come through with flying colors.

A brother, Dr. Robert Lathan, was a prominent ARP Minister, also a historian of note. He was author of a history of South Carolina, and also compiled sketches of the minister of the A.R.P.denomination. A son of Dr. Robert Lathan, Robert Lathan, Jr. was editor of the *Charleston News and Courier* and later of the *Asheville (NC) Daily Citizen*. In 1924 he was awarded the Pulitzer Prize for his famous editorial, "The Plight of the South Politically."

Mr. Lathan was Chester County's last, surviving Confederate veteran. He was actively engaged throughout the entire four years of the war with the exception of a few months while he was a prisoner in Baltimore recovering from a wound he sustained at Sharpsburg September 14, 1862.

Upon arriving in Chester in September 1872, Mr. Lathan took a position with Wylie, Roddey & Agurs, a large mercantile concern, as office man. Later he worked for George Melton in similar capacity, and later still he was Secretary and Treasurer of the Chester Manufacturing Company, now Springsteen Mill.

Mr. Lathan at the time of his death (March 8, 1939) lacked slightly less than two months of having attained his 97th birthday. He was indeed "Chester's Grand Old Man". He was a lifelong member of the A.R.P. church, a Sabbath school teacher for 64 years and a member of the Session for nearly as long.

Chester was signally blessed in having a man of Mr. Lathan's stature as a citizen for nearly sixty seven years. The contributions of such a person to a community in all of its various ways is measureless. Of a man like Mr. Lathan, nature might well stand up and say, to all the world, "This was a man."

Dr. Lathan's "Scribbling" includes Handwritten Papers, Newspaper Articles, Interviews

....."Spending a morning in the company with Mr. Lathan, of Chester, is better than keeping company with the best history books...."

McCONNELLSVILLE

Recollections of Noted York County Neighborhood.

EARLY A BUSINESS AND SOCIAL CENTER

First Settlers Sold Their Cotton and Did Their Business in Columbia—Building of the Railroad—First Business Houses—Anecdotes of Revs. Lowry Wilson and Henry R. Dickson—The First Physicians.

By S. B. Lathan.

About half way between Chester and Yorkville, or to be more accurate, twelve miles north of Chester and ten miles south of Yorkville on the Carolina and North-Western railroad, the prosperous and progressive village of McConnellsville is located. It got its name from Reuben McConnell, the father of the late Capt. John D. McConnell, who lived about two hundred yards south of the present station. I think the house is still standing, surrounded by some large oaks.

The residents of this section of York county in the early part of the last century, were to a great extent the ancestors of the present citizenship, viz.: The Loves, McConnells, Moores, Ashes, Lindsays McKnights, Burrises, McCleaves. The lands were thought to be better suited to growing the cereals than cotton, consequently, a great deal

Example of newspaper article

Samuel Boston Lathan

OFFICE OF S. B. LATHAN, COTTON BUYER.

Chester, S. C., _____ 190_

The 17th S.C. Reg't. C.S.A. to which I belonged was made up of 1 comp. from Lancaster, 4 from York, 2 from Fairfield, 1 from Chester & 2 from Barnwell Counties — J.H. Means former Gov. of S.C. was the first Col., F.W. McMaster Lt-Col. & Julius Mills Maj — These Companies first rendezvous near Colombia S.C. at what was known as Lightwood Knot Springs & there were organized into a Reg't with the above field officers & after a short while they were ordered to Charleston S.C. or rather Johns Island near there, at this latter place I joined Co D. of the Reg't about 1st March 1862 — We remained on the Island until some time in May when we moved Camp to near Rantowles on the Savannah & Charleston R.R. on account of the health of the Reg't — We were engaged mostly in picket duty while on the Island & also while at Rantowles. During April we had a slight engagement with the enemies cavalry near Legareville on Wadamalaw Island — our Comp. had two men wounded — but not seriously — this was our first time under fire of musketry

Example of handwritten papers

Our Early Settlers

Some of the pioneers who opened up Chester County – The Rocky Creek Settlement.

The country around Blackstock was settled by Scotch-Irish who emigrated from the Cumberland Valley of Pennsylvania and with others who joined them from the North of Ireland. It might be interesting to a few to know what constituted a "Scotch Irishman." I will go back to the beginning. During the reign of James I, a great many Scotch, went over from Scotland to North Ireland to build up its waste places and during the reign of Charles II and James II, a great number of others fled to the same place to avoid persecution at home. All these, while pure Scotch, came to be known as "Scotch Irish." They all belonged to the Presbyterian family. Persecution followed them to their adopted home, and a great many of their descendants sailed for America and formed a colony in Pennsylvania, in what is known as Bucks, York, Lancaster, and Chester counties. These were added to by immigrants from the Old Country from time to time until the colony embraced nearly all of the Cumberland Valley of Pennsylvania.

Parties drifted from this colony into Maryland, Virginia and the two Carolinas, forming settlements in all these states as far as Broad River in South Carolina. One of these settlements was in the southeastern portion of Chester county and the northern part of Fairfield county about fifteen miles from the present town of Chester, and was known as Little Rocky Creek. This settlement was supplemented from time to time from the colony in Pennsylvania and, also by recruits from the Mother Country, until it became a permanent fixture.

When Wm. Sayle in 1670 with a colony began the settlement of what is now known as South Carolina, this portion of the country was the mutual possession of the wild beast of the forest and, equally wild, Red Man. About the year 1732 this region began to be settled by white men. Some Scotch traders about this time established a trading post with the Indians near the mouth of Little Rocky Creek.

After Braddock's defeat in 1755 a great many from the Pennsylvania colony came south and some cast their lot with this colony which had grown to include nearly all of the eastern portion of Chester county. The first house of worship, or as it was then called, "Meeting House," was built of logs and stood near where the present Catholic Presbyterian church stands. While these people were all Presbyterian, they were of many sects, some Convenanters, conformist, non-conformist, associates, etc. But all a unit on Westminster Confession of Faith and Catechism. They for the time buried their differences and built this house of worship and called it Catholic. Most of the preaching was by missionaries from Scotland, Ireland or from the northern colonies. The British burnt this church during the Revolutionary war. After the war was over each of these sects having been greatly increased in numbers from the Mother Country, formed congregations and built churches of their own. The Covenanters, the Richmond Meeting house, the Associates, Hopewell and the Presbyterians Catholic. The peculiar circumstances in which they had been born and lived made them hate tyranny and love and long for liberty, so when the rupture came between the colonies and Great Britain, they cast their fortunes with the colonists, almost to a man, and many of them made the supreme sacrifice in order that their descendants might enjoy liberty and freedom of conscience, for which their ancestors had to flee their native land.

After the close of the Revolutionary War and the Treaty of Peace was signed between United States and Great Britain, a flood of immigrants came from the North Ireland. Schools were opened up, churches built and everything moved along smoothly, peace and prosperity reigned. The few Loyalists that remained made themselves very scarce.

Everything looked lovely but, "The best laid schemes of men and mice, gang-aft-agley."

The invention of the cotton gin revolutionized the cotton industry. Slave labor which had hitherto been confined mostly to the low country began to encroach on the small freeholder in the up country. Large plantations were being gradually augmented by the small land holders selling out. This continued slowly until 1832 when Nullification became an issue in South Carolina. This and the slavery question got into the churches and in one year thirty-two families sold out and moved to the Northwest. These homesteads were occupied by the slaves of the purchasers. Another big "going West" took place in 1840 with about the same result namely: Negro slaves taking the place of the small white farmer.

The war of 1861 came after that new era in this section.

This is a concrete account of the Rocky Creek settlement without any attempt at details or particulars.

I will now give some facts about persons and happenings in the immediate vicinity of Blackstock. I will not be particular as to the chronological order, but will take them up as they occur in my mind.

Long Forgotten Worthies.

A man of some prominence in the Blackstock community prior to the Civil War was James Young, or as he was better know as, Master Young. He taught school for many years not far from Hopewell A. R. P. church, and in his day was considered a fine teacher. His instruction embraced only reading, writing, arithmetic and surveying. Some few of his pupils studied Murray's English Grammar and Morse's Geography. He began his school on, or about the first of January, and continued six days in the week until the week before Christmas without any vacation. The only holidays were Saturdays before the celebration of the Lord's Supper at Hopewell church which was twice a year, and the Tuesday of the spring term of court for Chester county. He was never married and made his home at the Rev. John Hemphill's, then pastor of Hopewell church.

Alexander Skelly afterward taught a school about two miles northeast of Blackstock. He was regarded as a fine scholar, and well up in the ancient languages and higher mathematics, but was very visionary, was captain of the military company, and wrote a great deal of doggerel poetry, some of very good rhyme. One of his poems, "The Fourth of July", was fine in sentiment, and fairly good poetry. But as I have said he was visionary. Being endowed by nature with splendid mechanical trend of mind he conceived the idea that perpetual motion was a possibility and in order to demonstrate this idea, he built a small shop and went to work on his machine which was a very complex affair. Got the old ladies of the neighborhood to spin yarn to be used for a driving band. When he had all things completed he invited in his neighbors to see it work off, all things being in readiness. He pulled a lever to put his machine in gear and let on the power, but there was nothing doing. After tinkering a short while with it he again put on his so-called power with the same result, then he called some of the men standing around to assist in turning the driving wheel when the band broke to the chagrin of Skelly and the amusement of his visitors. This exploded Skelly's perpetual motion after the band broke. He walked off, and the building and machine rotted down.

The first school I ever attended was taught by William Douglas and was located just across and opposite to where W. H. Lathan now lives. He taught from the A. B. C.'s to the classics. In this day and time "grades" were unknown. The text books were very few. Webster's Blueback and Testament were the readers. Gough's Arithmetic, Smith's English Grammar and Morse's Geography constituted the text books. Some studied Peter Parley's history. The A. B. C. fellows had the alphabet in all its form pasted on a board paddle and this was used to teach them the letters. After they knew all the letters then they were promoted to Webster's Blueback, spelling and pronouncing in two letters, then three or four, when they got to "Baker" and on until words of nine or ten syllables could be spelled and pronounced correctly. When this was accomplished a boy or girl generally was a fair reader. Generally the last thing the whole school was asked was a spelling lesson in which they were given half an hour to prepare. This was done by the larger scholars getting their Walker's dictionaries and small ones the Blueback, studying or rather singing the words in a loud tone of voice, swinging their bodies back and forth keeping time. The seats were made of puncheons, smooth on one side and legs put in them. Some higher, some lower to suit the scholars. On these a small chap had to sit for hours with nothing to rest his back against.

The writing was all done with a quill pen. These were all made by the teacher. A scholar would obtain a quill from a goose wing and bring it to school and the teacher would transform it into a pen. These wrote much smoother than the present day stub pens, which were unknown then. They would not last more than a couple of days. Many who attended this – their names are now unknown in this section, viz: McCants, Perrys, Clarks, Ingrams, Knights, Sullivans, Goodrums, etc. My brother William and myself are the only ones now living that I know of.

At the Bell place about a mile above Blackstock formerly lived John F. DeBardelaben. I think he built the present dwelling on this place. I think he had studied medicine in his younger days, but never did any practicing. He ran a small farm. But his chief occupation was merchandising and keeping a house for the entertainment of travelers, and also a place where the stage drivers changed horses on their trips. He amassed considerable property for that day. One incident occurred in the neighborhood that created quite a commotion in that day and time. A great many peddlers plied their business by traveling the country, hauling their merchandise which consisted of a few dry goods, notions and watches and cheap jewelery, etc. One of these peddlers took sick at the house of Frank Elliott, who lived in the neighborhood. After being sick there for three days, Elliott told the man he must let him call in some men and have his money counted and his wares inventoried as he might die. This the peddler refused to do saying the only friend he had was his money, and got out of bed and went to DeBardelaben's. Some short time after some person, who possibly held a grudge against DeBardelaben, circulated a report that the peddler had died at DeBardelaben's and that he had appropriated all money and stuff to his use, and had buried the body of the peddler in a well in front of his dwelling and filled the well up. This for a short time created turmoil in the surrounding community, but after investigation it all turned about to be a myth.

About one mile west of the DeBardelaben place on Lee's Creek lived Wm. McKeown or as he was better known, Dr. Billy McKeown. He was above the average man in intelligence. His knowledge of medicine consisted in the botanical practice. He was also a surveyor and a millwright. As a surveyor he was considered an authority. He never made a survey of land in a haphazard way. Most of his calculations were made by Latitude and Departure and if the balance was not close he would resurvey until he did get an accurate balance. He possessed a great deal of botanical knowledge and could tell to which species most of the flowers and herbs in his section belonged. Also their medicinal properties. He did most of the bleeding in his section. This was very common in his day. When a person had fever, pneumonia and such diseases about the first thing that was done was to bleed him. The mode was to tie a cord tightly around the arm above the elbow so as to stop the flow of the venous blood, let the patient hold that arm outstretched with a staff to support it, then puncture the large vein and the blood would flow in a stream. When the patient began to show signs of fainting the ligature was removed and the patient put to bed. Dr. McKeown was especially known to me as a dentist. He extracted teeth for all that section, and when I was a small boy one for me, which made an indelible impression on my mind. I had been suffering for about a week with toothache and father decided it ought to be extracted. One of my sisters took me to Dr. Billy McKeown. When I got there the toothache was better, but I had been sent to have it pulled and the job had to be done.

Dr. McKeown pulled off his coat, rolled up his sleeves, washed his hands, got out his instrument and made ready for business. The instrument was a long piece of iron with an adjustable hook fixed in the side near its end. After padding the bar of iron where the hook was fastened, I was placed in a chair, my sister held my arms behind my back, Dr. McKeown placed the hook over the tooth and his hand upon my head and then well–

I fared at his hands much better than my good friend, Sam Tom McKeown, did on a like occasion, for in going through the same operation for him–after adjusting the hook and having no one to hold his hands he laid Sam Tom on his back on the floor and got astride of him to keep him still until the operation was over.

There was one virtue this old cant hook had, and that was it never broke a tooth off. It always brought out the tooth and not infrequently a piece of the jaw bone.

S. B. Lathan
Chester, S. C.
Aug. 5, 1921

Blackstock Reminiscences

Mr. S. B. Lathan Tells of Others Who Lived in That Community Many Years Ago

A noted man in the Blackstock vicinity was Dr. John Douglas—he was a native of Sumter county and after finishing his medical course located in this section and practiced his profession all his life, possibly 40 years. His wife was a Miss Lunsford, a daughter of Capt. Lunsford, who was buried in the Capital grounds near the State House in Columbia. He was a successful practitioner, and was frequently called into consultation by physicians at a distance. In 1854 an epidemic of scarlet fever broke out in this section. He told me that during this epidemic he went a whole week without ever undressing or sleeping in a bed. And that of all his patients, possibly 25 or 30, he did not lose a case. His principal treatment was sulphur. He told me once that when he was a student reading medicine most of the text books were printed in Latin. He was considered a fine surgeon. Although surgery had not at that time attained to its present proficiency, he nevertheless performed successfully some operations which required as much skill as any of the present day. The use of anaesthetics, such as ether, chloroform, cocaine, etc., were practically unknown and unused by doctors prior to 1850 in operating on a patient, especially in village and rural practice. When an arm or any other limb, in fact, when any surgical operation was to be made the patient was securely strapped on a table. Some stimulant, most frequently French brandy, was administered to the patient, and then the operator went to work. If he was of a tender and sympathetic nature his nerves would be excited by the groans and begging of the patient if they were of tender years. There was no trained nurses in those days and the sanitary conditions of the sick room would be considered almost criminal at this day and time. No precaution was taken to prevent the spread of the disease, consequently when one member of a family developed tuberculosis, typhoid fever or other contagious disease it generally went through the whole family. In the treatment of fever the patient was not allowed to drink any water–at intervals a teaspoonful would be given to keep the mouth and lips moist. And if a dose of calomel had been taken the patient was not allowed to taste water for twenty-four hours. Feeling the pulse was the method of ascertaining the temperature of the patient.

Dr. Douglas had–why I don't know–a colony of Indians on his plantation near his home. For these he built comfortable houses, and had the children schooled at his own expense. During the Civil War I think they went back to where they came from. He never succeeded in getting the Indians out of them. The women made earthen pottery, and the men ate and slept.

At the outbreak of the Civil War Dr. Douglas was appointed surgeon of the 6th Reg., S. C., but owing to his inability to ride horseback, resigned and came home and died in 1867. If I remember correctly, he had four sons, who practiced medicine. The oldest, Lunsford, was a man of brilliant intellect and progressive ideas. He wrote several pamphlets pertaining to agriculture. Such as soil preservation and upbuilding–rotation in crops. One especially on swine breeding which did more to improve the breed of hogs in Chester county than had ever been thought of before. He supplanted the old "razor back" with the Berkshire and Corbet breed. He died from an accident in the prime of his life, shortly after being elected to the legislature from Chester county by the largest vote ever received by any candidate up to this time.

Dr. John Douglas, while his practice was very extensive yet was not lucrative to him. He practiced medicine not for the dollars and cents alone which were in it but to relieve suffering. He would get out of bed on a cold winter night and answer a call to the poorest family in the neighborhood as knowing he would never receive a cent for his visit as readily as if called to the richest. On a bright April morning one of his daughters married Dr. H. H. Hicklin who practiced medicine near Sharon in York county. One Eli Harrison of Longtown, Fairfield county, one Mr. Moore, of Texarkana, Tex., and Miss Fannie, the youngest, married Wm. Thorn and now lives at the old homestead. His four sons were all doctors and are all dead, leaving no families, consequently there is none of his descendants that bears the name of Douglas. As a postscript, I would say physicians in that time carried their medicine with them and never wrote a prescription to a drug store to be filled. Dr. Douglas told me the first patient he had was an old black woman suffering from dropsy and he was called in after the other doctors had about abandoned her, and in less than a week the old woman died, which incident gave him a send off, as they knew there was virtue in his medicine.

The first R. R. agent was named Collins, or to more fully express it, Charles Henry Bolingbrook Collins, of Columbia SC. There was nothing notable about him. He was small of stature, had black hair and sported a huge mustache. After the depot was located there the postoffice was located in this and the agent ran both. For some time after the completion of the railroad there was no Sabbath day traffic. Either by passenger or freight trains. The passenger trains made the trip from Columbia to Charlotte and vice versa every day except Sabbath day leaving Columbia about half past eight A. M. and get to Charlotte at five P. M. The stops were more and longer, viz., at Winnsboro and Chester the stop was 20 minutes. At stations like Blackstock, 5 minutes; Cornwell was the dinner house and it made a stop there of 25 minutes. I don't think they had any connections to make at either terminals. One of the conductors was named Fowler and I think was from the Feasterville section of Fairfield county. I can't recall the other. There were no ticket agents. The conductor collected all fares from passengers, which was five cents per mile, or two dollars and fifty cents from Columbia to Blackstock. The engineer always blew his whistle twice before leaving a station to give the passengers warning he was going to start. At Columbia half an hour before leaving the engineer would blow what was known as the "long blow" to warn those who expected to get aboard that the train would leave in thirty minutes. The train was composed of first and second class coaches or rather a coach in which ladies and their attendants, such as husband and wife, brother and sister, or gentleman and lady, as traveling companions were only admitted. The other coach was reserved for stags, or gentlemen not accompanied with a lady. There was no Negro travel, except nurses to look after children and they rode in the ladies' car as this coach was called–also a combination coach for the baggage and such. The conductors had the authority to give return tickets, for example if a passenger wanted to go to some place and return the same day, he would tell the conductor and he gave him a return ticket. This road was originally known as the Columbia & Charlotte R. R. which were the terminals of it. The extension to Augusta was not built until 1870. The stockholders consisted to a great extent of persons living in Columbia and Charlotte and citizens of the counties through which the road ran. And prior to the Civil War always paid the stockholders a seven per cent dividend. The annual meeting of the stockholders was usually held in Columbia and all stockholders and their families got free rides to the place of meeting. Some families increased considerably on these occasions. These meetings were not mere formalities, but the officers had to come across and make everything clear to these rural stockholders. The president, superintendent, treasurer and directors, the latter two from each county through which the road ran were at these meetings.

When Sherman's army passed through South Carolina, they destroyed the road as far as Blackstock, after the war the stockholders bonded the road and rebuilt the torn-up part, but owing to the high price of material and construction and the poor traffic both in passenger and freight business, it soon defaulted in payment of interest on bonds, was sold and thus passed out of the hands of the original builders and owners.

S. B. Lathan.
Chester, SC, Aug. 15, 1921.

This same article appeared in the *Yorkville Enquirer* "Sulphar cure for Scarlet Fever", August 1926

The Old Time Militia

Very Elaborate Organization, But Poorly Equipped–Mr. Lathan's Reminiscences.

Prior to the Civil War South Carolina had a well organized militia composed of divisions, brigades, battalions, and companies, each having their territorial boundaries fixed by statute. Chester county had one regiment and two battalions, the latter known as the eastern and western, and each commanded by a Major. The Senior Major ranked as Lieutenant Colonel. Every company had its territorial boundary, somewhat resembling the present day township or school district. These companies were required by law to meet at some designated place once every two months for drill. At the first meeting, generally in January, all company officers were elected from Captain to corporal. Frequently the same officers would be re-elected. The company was then divided into "Beats," and one of the men appointed leader in the respective "Beats." The purpose of this division was to do patrol duty, which was required of all male citizens between the ages of 18 and 45, also of all slave-holders irrespective of age. This patrol was a kind of vigilance committee who would visit Negro houses and see that no Negroes were there except those living on the place or had written permission from and to which the bearer had permission of the owner to go and the time limit in which to return. Usually Negro men who had families living on a different plantation were given passes from Saturday night until Monday morning. Any Negro could get a pass unless he wanted to go out on a chicken hunt or something else of the kind.

At the next regular meeting of the company, the leader, or as he was called the captain of the patrol, had to make a certified report that he and his squad had performed this duty, when another squad was appointed and so on. Preachers, practicing physicians and school teachers were the only ones exempted from patrol duty.

As to the military feature of this organized militia, it was a mere farce. The privates never wore any uniforms, the arms were of all kinds, single barrel shot guns, squirrel rifles, etc., and these were only used at regimental drills and, then only semi-occasionally. The commissioned officers on regimental and battalion drill had to appear in full uniform, which consisted of white pants and blue frock coats with brass buttons galore, and swords. The captains had epaulets on each shoulder, Lieutenant one on the right shoulder, the Colonel and Major in addition wore cocked hats with large red and white plumes, top boots and brass spurs, and when mounted on prancing steeds made a spectacular appearance. When all the Captains had gotten their companies lined up and formed in a straight line, a courier was dispatched to notify the Colonel who would then come on the field and take command of the regiment. The muster grounds were generally an old field. The crowd was kept off the grounds by men selected for this duty and were known to the populace as dog-pelters. After marching and counter marching, double quicking, etc., for a couple of hours, the regiment was formed into a hollow square when the Colonel would make a speech complimenting the officers and men on their proficiency. Some times his speech would be on some live question of the day; such as politics, education or something of the like nature, and after he had finished would turn over the command to the company officers and ride off the field.

A very amusing incident occurred at one of these drills. Col. Atkinson when in command of the regiment, had carefully prepared a written speech for the occasion. By some means Buck Massey got possession of this manuscript and memorized it and on the day of the muster, by previous arrangement with some of his "pals," when the crowd had assembled and before the drill, was vociferously called on for a speech, and mounting a box at once proceeded to deliver the Colonel's speech. When the drill was over the Colonel was minus a speech and quietly dismissed the regiment and rode off the field.

One thing about these musters which was especially interesting to the country boy, was the old black mother with her ginger cakes and cider. I can remember yet how good they tasted when hungry, and how she would smile when she got ten cents pay for a cup of cider and one of these big ginger cakes.

Whiskey was plentiful and always in evidence among a certain class, and when they got tanked up fights would be in order, but, I will say to their credit, they never used knives or pistols, but fought it out fist and skull, consequently, none was seriously hurt. I remember, though quite a small boy, they had a regular championship fight. A Mr. Gill was the bully of the eastern battalion and a Mr. Hardin of the western and, to decide which was the better man they determined to fight it out. A large ring was circumscribed on the ground, each battalion marched up its man, who pulled off their coats, vests, and collars, rolled up their sleeves, stepped in the ring and the crowd gathered around crying "fair play," and the slugging commenced. After pounding, choking and gouging for some time, one of them said he had enough and the fight ended. After washing their faces and patching up their wounds, they shook hands and made friends, and the championship was decided.

S. B. Lathan.
Chester, S. C., Aug. 30, 1921.

The Textile Industry

Mr. S. B. Lathan Tells of First Spinning Mill in Chester County- A Crude, But Serviceable Affair.

One of the many changes in the South caused by the results of the Civil War was the evolution of the textile industry, which hitherto had almost exclusively been confined to the New England States.

The first fulling mill operated south of Virginia was built near the mouth of Fishing Creek where it empties into the Catawba river, in Chester county. This mill was built about the year 1788, and was used for dyeing, fulling and pressing the cloth woven by the persons in this vicinity, and was said to have been done in a very satisfactory manner. This was at first confined entirely to woolen cloth but gradually extended its operations to cotton cloth.

In the early part of the 19th century, nearly every family had its spinning wheel and hand loom. There were two varieties of spinning wheels. One operated by hand while the operator walked back and forth drawing out the thread. After the style of mule spinning, this required very little skill to operate it and was mostly used by black women to spin yarn to be woven into cloth for the slaves on the larger plantations, and also to utilize the labor of the black woman during the winter months. The other variety was operated by foot power and was used mostly by a white woman sitting by the side of the wheel and working it with her feet, like working a sewing machine. This made a much smoother and finer yarn than the other wheel. After the yarn was spun it was then reeled off the spools by a hand reel into banks and then taken to a warper, and finally to the loom where it was woven. A good weaver could weave about four yards in a day of plain cloth throwing one shuttle, or, if woolen jeans with two shuttles, two to three yards.

The raw wool and cotton were carded into rolls with hand cards about a foot and four inches wide, equipped with wire teeth. One of these was held stationary on the knee and cotton or wool was placed on its teeth, with the other this was carded until the fibers were straightened out, then it was taken off in a roll. The carder could card about as many of these rolls as a spinner could spin.

In the early 50' Mr. Daniel McCullough built a spinning mill on Catawba river near where the Republic Cotton Mills now stands. The Fingerville Mill in Spartanburg county and the old Saluda Mill in Lexington county antedated this mill a few years. Mr. McCullough operated this by water power obtained from the Catawba River. The operators were all slaves from his plantation except the superintendent and heads of the different departments and the cotton used for spinning was chiefly grown on his own plantation. The yarns produced were coarse, numbers 8's, 10's, and 12's, and were put up in five and ten pound bales, which he peddled out through Chester and adjoining counties, selling to the merchants who in turn sold them to the different families to be woven into cloth. This yarn was mostly used for warps, the filling being spun in these homes on spinning wheels.

A bale of cotton at this time weighed about 300 pounds.

This mill was a very crude affair in comparison with the present day cotton mill. It did not use more than three hundred bales of cotton in a year, but paid Mr. McCullough a very good profit on his raw cotton. When Sherman's army passed through this section in 1865 it was burned together with everything else in his line of march. Mr. McCullough died shortly after and the mill was never rebuilt. This property finally fell into the possession of the Southern Power Company and now the Republic Cotton Mills, a magnificent manufacturing plant stands in a few hundred yards of where the McCullough mill stood.

A wonderful evolution from the fulling mill to McCullough's Mill and now the Great Falls hydro-electric plant and Republic Mills, now using as much cotton in a week as the McCullough factory did in a whole year. The home spinning and weaving gradually grew into disuse, especially in making white cloth as a better article could be bought comparatively cheap. A few plantations kept it up to utilize the labor of black women during the winter months. The smaller farmers who generally kept a flock of sheep, the wool of which was spun and woven into homemade jeans, blankets and knit into socks. These jeans were durable and warm and clothed all the male members comfortably during the winter. Very few store clothes were used by these sturdy toilers of the farm and yeomen of the country. After South Carolina seceded from the Union, war was declared and we were shut out from the rest of the world commercially. The only way to replenish the wardrobe was to do so within ourselves, consequently, the old spinning wheels were brought out of the garrets and outhouses where many of them had been stored away as relics of the past and pressed into service. Those who could spin and weave went to work with a vim, those who could not learned the business, and, as a result a spinning wheel and loom were as common in the homes as knives and forks.

The ladies all from patriotic motive or necessity wore homespun dresses. Many of them spun, woven and made by their own hands. Men's wear came under the same rule. This was one time that everybody was on an equality as to dress.

After the war the spinning wheel and loom were soon discarded and today can only be found as curios in a few homes. Many of the younger set of today never saw one of these wheels or looms on which their grandmothers spun or wove the clothing for the family.

S. B. Lathan.
Chester, S. C., Sept. 12, 1921.

Hopewell A. R. P. Church

Interesting Sketch of Historic Old Church–Preaching In the Neighborhood As Early As 1775.

About three miles north-east of Blackstock in Chester county, where the public road leading to Chester crosses the one leading to Cornwell, stands Hopewell A. R. P. church. The exact date when this congregation was organized is not definitely known. Rev. Thomas Clark preached in this neighborhood occasionally as early as 1775, as there were several Seceders at this date living in this neighborhood. The place of preaching was in a grove at the south-west corner of the present grave yard. After the Revolutionary War broke out there was very little preaching anywhere in the surrounding country. The only minister in this section at this time was Rev. William Martin and he was for a long time a prisoner of war in the hands of the British.

In the year 1783 Rev. John Jamison preached occasionally in the bounds of this congregation and possibly other ministers. In 1787 Rev. John Lind did missionary work in this community, and very likely organized the church. In the following year, 1788, Rev. John Boyce was sent out by the Associate Reformed Presbytery of Pennsylvania to do missionary work in North and South Carolina. He labored as stated supply to the congregations of Hopewell, SC, and Coddle Creeks, Gilead and Prosperity, NC. When he first came into this neighborhood he preached at a log house located near Edward McDaniel's. This house was used jointly by the Covenanters and Seceders.

During the year 1788 Mr. Boyce began preaching at the stand or grove (Hopewell). The arrangement between the several congregations of which he was stated supply was that Hopewell should have half of his ministerial services.

In 1789 the first house of worship at Hopewell was built. It was a log house and stood near the north-west corner of the graveyard. The work of erecting this building was done by the male members of the congregation, and it is said all the logs of the building were hewed by Mr. Samuel Moffatt, then a younger man and the only one in this community who knew how to use a broadaxe. Mr. Moffatt afterward became a ruling elder in Hopewell and died in 1805.

Rev. John Boyce was probably installed pastor of Hopewell, Coddle Creek, Prospect and Gilead sometime during the year 1790. His pastorate lasted only a few years. He died March 18th, 1793. His mortal remains were buried in Hopewell graveyard. An unpretentious stone marks the spot. It is probable he did little preaching during the year 1793.

He boarded with David McQuiston, who lived on Little River in the bounds of what is now New Hope congregation. There is a tradition that one of Mr. David McQuiston's daughters and Mr. Boyce were engaged to be married and that during his last illness she tenderly nursed him and soothed his brow on his dying pillow. A short while after the death of Mr. Boyce Miss Margaret McQuiston died, and her mortal remains were buried by the side of Mr. Boyce.

In 1791 the first bench of Elders was chosen, viz:

James Chestnut, William McQuiston and James Meek. James Dunn, David McQuiston and Thomas McDill having been Elders in Ireland had been acting in this capacity at Hopewell ever since its organization in 1787.

After the death of Mr. Boyce they were without a pastor until 1795, but were occasionally visited and preached to by Revs. Jas. Rodgers, Peter McMullen and William Blackstocks. Although Hopewell was a vacancy it continued to increase very rapidly. During the month of February, 1795, Rev. John Hemphill, who had been sent in 1794 by the first Presbytery of Pennsylvania as a missionary to the South, began preaching at Hopewell but after a short while returned to Greencastle, Pennsylvania. About the time of his departure the people of Hopewell, Union and Little River (now New Hope) united in presenting to him a call to become their pastor, but he held it for consideration. After his return to Pennsylvania Rev. Jas. McKnight preached at Hopewell. During the summer of 1795 Mr. Hemphill concluded to accept the call presented to him by the congregation of Hopewell, Union and Little River and made known the fact by letter to Rev. James Rodgers, which he read to the congregation at Hopewell from the pulpit. The Hopewell people at once made arrangements to move their pastor from Pennsylvania to South Carolina. Two young men, a Mr. Strong and Mr. McQuiston set out for Greencastle. Each rode one horse and led another. In a wagon which they purchased in Pennsylvania they hauled the effects of their pastor to South Carolina, Mr. Hemphill and his wife riding through on horse back and carrying a small child a distance of over five hundred miles.

Up to this time all three of these congregations were embraced in one and known as Hopewell, while there was a stand in western Hopewell called Kerneyham from the name of an individual who lived in the vicinity of New Hope. Nevertheless, Hopewell was the only church. It was different in the Union congregation as they had no organization as a congregation until Mr. Hemphill's visit in 1795.

The pastorate of Rev. John Hemphill began in the fall of 1795 and lasted until the 30th day of May, 1830 – when he died.

During Mr. Hemphill's pastorate in the year 1800 the second house of worship was built. It was a brick structure forty by fifty feet, hipped roofed, walls plastered, floors of brick, with a gallery on the sides reached by a stairway from the outside – the pulpit was elevated about six feet and inclosed with a balustrade. It was reached by a narrow stairway. Overhead was a sounding board. The seats were very close together with high straight backs and the aisles narrow. There was no way of heating the building, although there was a small one room house near the church called the Session house in which was a fire place and on cold mornings a log fire at which ladies with small children could warm after probably riding four or five miles to church horseback. Hopewell on the death of Mr. Hemphill, May, 1830, was for the second time without a pastor. In November, 1832, Rev. Warren Flenniken was installed pastor of Hopewell and Union, New Hope having formed a union with the Brick church in Fairfield county and called Rev. Jas. Boyce as pastor. Mr. Flenniken continued to preach at Hopewell three-fourths of his time until 1839 when Union united with Tirzah in York county and became the pastorate of Rev. L. McDonald, Hopewell taking all the time of Mr. Flenniken.

During the pastorage of Mr. Flenniken Hopewell passed through a critical period. The slavery question and the doctrine of nullification began to be agitated, neighbor was arrayed against neighbor, family against family and in some cases individuals in the same family – this started a tide of emigration west and in little over a year seventy-five members left and went west.

In 1849 Mr. Flenniken demitted his pastorage and on May 31st, 1850, Rev. R. W. Brice was installed pastor of Hopewell.

During the time between the resignation of Mr. Flenniken and the installation of Mr. Brice the congregation was supplied by Rev. Thos. Kitchin. He never let anything prevent him from filling his appointments and was always at the church whether wet or cold on the day he was to preach and rarely preached a sermon under an hour long.

When Mr. Brice commenced his pastorate, all the difference among the members, which had existed in the latter part of Mr. Hemphill's time and during all of Mr. Flenniken's had completely passed away and peace and harmony prevailed throughout the congregation. In 1854 a new house of worship was erected and furnished in good style. This is the third house erected since the organization of the congregation. It is a frame building fifty by seventy feet with comfortable seats and well arranged for heating. The pastorage of Mr. Brice lasted until March, 1878, when he died. During the ministry of Mr. Brice probably fifty Black people were members in good standing in the church. All of these after the close of the Civil War drifted away to churches of their own. Also during the Civil War a great many of the young men of Hopewell were either killed in battle, or died in hospitals from wounds or disease. The first member killed in battle was William McDill. He fell at the battle of Dranesville December 20, 1861.

In March, 1879, one year after the death of Mr. Brice Rev. John A. White was installed pastor and continued to preach faithfully and acceptably to the people of Hopewell until May, 1911, when death suddenly ended his faithful services.

After his death J. Lewis White, a son of Rev. John White and a student in the Due West Theological seminary, supplied the church. The congregation had extended a call to him, but on account of his health he was never installed, dying.

There have gone out from this congregation reared either partly or in whole within its fold 22 young men who became preachers of the everlasting gospel and now after nearly one hundred and fifty years Hopewell is still in a flourishing condition.

All the foregoing pastors are buried in the adjoining graveyard.

S. B. Lathan.
Chester, S. C., Oct. 4, 1921.

The U. C. V. Dinner and Some Recollections of Woodward

Editor Reporter: - On Wednesday, the 11th instant, about fifteen veterans, of the C. S. A., by special invitation of the Catherine Ladd Chapter, U. D. C., assembled at the home of Mr. Tom Brice, near Woodward to enjoy a dinner given in their honor. In this number, four States were represented, viz., Virginia, North Carolina, South Carolina, and Mississippi. These dinners are an annual event of this Chapter, but the present one was somewhat different from all the former ones. Heretofore they were given in the form of a general picnic. Everybody who wished came, and as a natural result the object and prime intent (honoring the old veteran) was beginning to occupy a second place at these functions. Consequently, this Chapter hit upon a happy solution and this year gave the dinner at the home of one of the Daughters and sent written invitations to the veterans in the counties of Fairfield and Chester.

About 11 o'clock the invited guests, viz., the C. S. A. veterans, began to assemble at the beautiful home of Mr. Tom Brice, situated in a magnificent grove, with a yard fragrant with many flowers and the building equipped with all modern conveniences.

As the veterans arrived they were met and greeted by some one of the Daughters, and introduced to other members of the Chapter.

After being comfortably seated – the old fellows passed the time in relating and reviewing their war experiences to each other, which was tinged with sadness and joy. One o'clock, the dinner hour, having arrived we were all invited into the dining room where a sumptuous feast was spread. I can't conceive how it could be improved upon either in quality, service or quantity. The members of the Chapter acted as waiters and were careful that no one was overlooked. This Chapter does not do things by halves, but showed the same spirit as their fathers and brothers did in camp and on the battle-fields, and no one would dare say that their fathers and brothers were "slackers."

While seated at the table, I found myself mentally asking, "Is the preparation of these viands and inviting us to pertake of them the only or prime motive of this occasion?" And I was forced to the conclusion that it was the expression of a deep-seated conviction to perpetuate and keep in the fore the valor and heroism and the hardships and suffering that their ancestors endured for a cause believed to be right. After everyone had eaten to the full of this bountiful feast we again assembled on the front porch, where cigars were passed around by the Daughters. Capt. John Lyles then gave an interesting account of the war activities of Catherine Ladd for whom this chapter is named. After giving a hearty vote of thanks to these ladies for their thoughtfulness and kindness, we broke up and made our way back home – with memories of the occasion that will last many days.

These chapters of the U. D. C. are doing a great work in preserving the history of the soldiers of the C. S. A, which is not contained in the written histories and in the years to come their minutes will be sought by the coming historians for the true history.

May they keep up the good work and ever keep in mind from whence they sprang.

Woodward is a by-product of Sherman. As is well known when Gen. Sherman made his march through South Carolina, he was very careless with fire, consequently he burned everything in his line of march. He tore and completely destroyed the railroad near the present location of Woodward. When the troops of Lee and Johnston were returning to their home, they were disembarked here and made their way to their respective homes by foot, going via Newberry. This was especially the case with the men from the western part of S. C. and the states west of South Carolina. This place, then an old straw field, was used for sometime as the rail road terminal - about 1866 Burr Rosborough, a former conductor of the railroad, opened a grocery store here and shortly after the railroad built a depot, the depot at Blackstock having been burnt by Sherman's men. This action on the part of R. R. authorities raised a howl from the Blackstock people and after much wrangling the depot building at Woodward, or as it was then known as Central, was torn down and moved to Blackstock, when the railroad was rebuilt to Columbia. The people in the Woodward section got busy and the railroad people reestablished this station under the name of Woodward in honor of W. R. Woodward, Sr., who lived near there.

In the meantime the mercantile business began to take on greater life and expansion. J. A. Brice & Co. did a tremendous lien business in a more or less haphazard way - credit was very cheap with them and as a consequence they lost heavily. I remember once in going through their store building and seeing the haphazard way they had their merchandise arranged - asked one of the clerks if they did not have a great many goods stolen. He replied no that there was no need for any one to steal as they could buy all they wanted on credit. Of course they failed. There are two firms here now doing a safe and profitable business, viz., T. W. Brice & Co. and W. M. Patrick, and also both firms are engaged in extensive farming interests.

Mr. Burr Rosborough ran the railroad agency in connection with his store at first, but a little later John McCarley became agent and when the depot was moved to Blackstock he became agent there after him.

A short distance from the depot on the eastern side on a beautifully elevated knoll Concord Presbyterian church is located. This is among the oldest churches in the county and tradition has it that after the Revolutionary War the different sects of the Presbyterian bodies established preaching places where it would be most convenient for them to attend. Some of these adherents had frequently to go some distance. In the case of Concord the location at first was some four or five miles east of the present location, but about 1785 they had this station or meeting house changed to the present location. The organization was consummated in April, 1796, when the Rev. Robert Walker, pastor Bethesda church, York district, was commissioned to organize these members into a church. The first elders were James Astor, James Caldwell, James Hindman and Abraham Miller. Rev. Wm. Rosborough was the first pastor. The membership increased rapidly after the organization, peace and harmony prevailed, until 1826 when Rev. Stadford of Virginia was installed pastor. He introduced Watts' hymns into the worship, to the exclusion of Rouse's version of David's Psalms. This raised a storm of protest. A great many members withdrew their membership, others would not open their mouths in praise while any human composition was being sung. It took the church a long time to get over its effects.

About the year 1849 Rev. J. R. Gilland became pastor. He was a fine scholar and about the same time that he became pastor opened an academy near by known as the Concord Academy. This was the only school in this section in which a young man or girl could be prepared for College and as a consequence was largely patronized. Mr. Gilland was very strict in its government and was a terror to idle and non-studious scholars but an inspiration to the studious. He left here and went to Williamsburg county. After this the academy lost its prestige and soon went out of commission.

In 1861 a great many of the young men volunteered and went to the war, many never to return, some of whose bodies are buried in the graveyard hard by. Others sleep in unknown graves on the battle fields where they gave their lives in defense of their country, awaiting the resurrection morning.

I have a great veneration for this old church, for here my mother in infancy had the water of baptism applied to her forehead, here in after years she gave herself to Christ, and continued in this church until 1829 when she married my father when she removed her membership to Hopewell A. R. P. church. The present brick building was erected I think in 1812.

Aware of the risk of worrying you and your readers I will note something in reference to some places and people in the vicinity of Woodward in the long ago:

About half a mile south there lived a man named John L. Young. Along in the 40's he was high sheriff of Fairfield county, and was a kind of boss in the community. His place was one at which the stage coaches relayed their teams, also it was an eating station. He ran a store, sold whiskey, which was common for stores at that time, also was postmaster. The office was named "Youngsville." At this place in 1851 a general camp muster at which all the militia of the upper part of South Carolina assembled. Also the cadets of the Citadel at Charleston and Arsenal of Columbia participated. Gen. R. G. M. Dunovant, late Colonel of the Palmetto regiment of Mexican fame, was commander-in-chief. The men were put through all tactics of regular war such as living in tents, guard mounting, company and regimental drills, etc. The cadets made a splendid appearance on drill. I never have seen better since. On the last day they fought a sham battle using blank cartridges. This resembled a real battle about as much as a cat resembles a dog. There came near being a great tragedy just after the battle was opened. A cannon that was being used burst when the second shot was fired, and fortunately there were not many near it, otherwise there would have been sure death to some, as the pieces were scattered with force in every direction. J. H. Means, who was then governor, was present with his staff. He made a speech to the men in which he praised them galore, and then launched in a political speech advocating secession.

When the company from Chester left for the Mexican war, they camped the first night at Youngsville. It left Chester on Saturday and marched this far the first day. I can well remember hearing the drum beating the next (Sabbath) morning as they were leaving Youngsville on the march, although quite small. I thought it was a great sin to be doing such things on the Sabbath day, and I haven't changed my mind as to that. Youngsville was head-quarters in the section for hog drovers. They would drive their hogs through from Tennessee and Kentucky – stop over possibly a week at a place and the owners of the large plantations would buy their meat to supply their Negroes, from them while, at the different places.

Youngsville, once the most noted place in this section, has become one of the "has beens" – all the old settlers around are gone and their lands are now owned by strangers.

S. B. Lathan.
Chester, S. C., Apr. 13, 1923.

Judge Thos. J. Mackey

Noted Character in Chester County 50 Years Ago – Soldier, Jurist, Raconteur – Had Few Equals as a Wit and a Conversationalist.

By S. B. Lathan.

During the Reconstruction period of South Carolina after the Civil War, one among the many of the heretofore unknown who came to the front was one, T. J. Mackey. I think he was a native of Lancaster county, as his parents went to Charleston in his early life; and I know nothing of his history until the breaking out of the Mexican War, when he volunteered and went as a private in the famous Palmetto Regiment and continued with the same until its return. He was severely wounded in the knee during the fighting around the fortifications of the City of Mexico. After his return home, the State of South Carolina gave him a free scholarship to the Citadel. This, I have heard, but am not positive as to his being educated by the State; at any rate he graduated from the Citadel.

Shortly after graduating he got an appointment under the United States Government as Civil Engineer in locating the public lands beyond the Mississippi River in Kansas, Nebraska, etc., which position he held until the secession of South Carolina, and the breaking out of the Civil War. Then he joined the Confederate Army and received a position on the staff of General Sterling Price, of the Confederate Army, as engineer, which position he held until the close of the war.

Upon the downfall of the Confederacy he returned to Charleston, and being of a nervous, excitable disposition, at once entered into ward politics and became a somewhat noted figure in the Radical party of the City of Charleston, and was appointed by Governor Scott as Trial Justice or Magistrate.

Possibly, it might be well for me to explain the situation after the Lee and Johnston surrender of the political situation in South Carolina for the few following years:

As soon as Lee and Johnston surrendered their armies, the United States Government placed military forces in nearly every town of any size in South Carolina. This was done, they said, as a precaution to keep down riots and pillaging generally through the country by the discharged soldiers. This military command also acted as a court between the Negroes and the white people. Afterwards the Freedmen's Bureau took charge, and provost guards were established at every court house, and the military officers in command acted as judge of all matters between the Negroes and the whites.

President Johnston appointed B. F. Perry Provisional Governor of South Carolina. Governor Perry called every county to elect representatives to the Legislature. These representatives met in Columbia, organized governments, accepted the

Fourteenth Amendment to the Constitution and elected judges, and at the same time that the delegates were elected, other civil officers for the State were elected, but unfortunately this Legislature passed a law known as the Black Code, which restricted the liberties of the Negro, also they chose delegates to go to Washington to negotiate the State's reception back into the Union. Congress refused to accept their terms; placed the State under military authority with General Canby stationed at Columbia, in command. In 1867 Canby ordered a registration of all the men, irrespective of color, to register as voters with a view of establishing a civil government. No man that had ever aided or abetted the Southern Confederacy, directly or indirectly, could take the oath required, consequently, very few white men could vote. The Negroes and the Carpet-baggers held the election, elected delegates to a State convention, adopted the Constitution, which was acceptable to the U. S. Government, and a general election was then held for Governor on down to all the minor officers, all the other old officers being ousted.

The Legislature elected a judge for the sixth circuit, George W. Williams, prominent lawyer of Yorkville. He declined to accept, because he was unwilling to associate with the other Radical judges that were elected, thereupon, they elected W. N. Thomas, of Union county, South Carolina, who served four years. At the expiration of his time, T. J. Mackey, then still a Trial Justice in Charleston, was elected judge of the sixth circuit. He then moved to Chester and made his home here as long as he remained in South Carolina.

While in Chester he became a prominent figure on the streets. He was a man of wonderful individuality, always wore a Prince Albert coat, high beaver hat, and walked with a gold-headed staff, and moved as if he was going to catch a train. It was not long until he was recognized head of the Radical party, which consisted mostly of Negroes in the county, and in all their processions he generally drove at the head of the column in the buggy floating a United States flag, and accompanied by some prominent Negro of the county. When any Radical conventions met at the court house he was chosen chairman, and ran the convention according to his ideas, and to suit himself. Some conventions were often very amusing, as several of the Negroes would want to make a speech at the same time and on different subjects, and sometimes, with considerable effort, he was hardly able to maintain order.

On one occasion, one delegate of African descent arose, addressing the chairman, and wanted to make a motion. Mackey replied: "The only motion you can made is towards the door, and you better get there pretty quick."

He always was chosen as a delegate to the State conventions, and had the other delegate chosen from some other member that he had absolute control of their votes when they got to Columbia.

When he first appeared on the bench he made a fairly good impression. He was not accredited at first of knowing much law, but being a very hard student soon made up this deficiency.

His circuit was composed of the counties of Fairfield, Chester, Lancaster, York, Union, and I think, Spartanburg. After serving some time as judge he might be classed as an Autocrat, Jurist and Wag. He ran the court absolutely according to his own notions, generally opened at half past nine or nine-thirty in the mornings, and adjourned whenever he felt like it. I know of one instance when he called a case on the docket for trial at twelve o'clock in the night, and he claimed by holding night sessions he could thus dispatch business faster, when often the juries, witnesses, and attorneys would have to go all day without dinner or supper, not knowing at what time they might be called. Some of his decrees for prominent cases, I have been told by lawyers, competent of judging, that they were as fine as any ever rendered in any court. At that time a judge could comment on the evidence, and this Mackey never neglected to do. Some of his comments of the testimony were very ludicrous.

I remember one case in which two prominent citizens of Chester county brought cross-suits for damages and each of their attorneys praised each of their clients for their good citizenship, high moral characters and truthfulness. Mackey, in his charge to the jury, used about the following language; "Gentlemen of the jury, in listening to the testimonies and the arguments of the learned counsel on both sides, I have no doubt you were reminded of walking through a cemetery and reading the epitaphs over the graves of the departed, and would be forced to the conclusion that none but the good die, so in listening to this testimony and argument, you may have come to the conclusion that none but the good citizens of the county get into lawsuits. You will weigh the testimonies, render your verdict, and may the Lord have mercy on your souls; let the record be given to the jury."

Then he always in sentencing prisoners was very unique in some of his sentences. On one occasion a gentlemen plead guilty, after having a mistrial in his case once or twice, to a technical assault and battery on an old drunken Negro, whom he kicked out of his place of business. The gentleman's attorney had seen Mackey and talked the case over with Mackey, and which Mackey was always willing to do with any lawyer, and he agreed if he would plead guilty that he would impose a nominal fine as a sentence. The party plead guilty, Mackey told him to stand up, and after giving him a lecture about assaulting an honorable citizen of African descent, etc., pronounced that the sentence of the court is, "That you serve ten years at hard labor in the penitentiary," and then stopped, looking around over the audience winking occasionally, said, "Or pay a fine of one dollar."

On one occasion in Lancaster county he abruptly dismissed the Grand Jury, because they failed to bring in an indictment against a party whom he wanted prosecuted, which, at the time, created considerable stir in the county.

On another occasion at Winnsboro, after charging the Grand Jury as to their duties, etc., he said, "It might be well for you to look into and investigate the boarding houses, as there is great probability of some of the boarders becoming martyrs at the "steak," and also to see whether certain domestic insects, better known as bed bugs, were not entitled to draw pensions from the United States Government on account of having drawn British blood during the time Cornwallis's Army was stationed there."

Also on an occasion in Chester during court, one Garland Smith, better known as "Wick" Smith, of Carmel Hill section, was indicted for beating up a notorious Negro in that section known as Ike Cassells. As Smith was found guilty of assault and battery, and being a veteran of the Mexican War, Mackey was friendly disposed towards him. In passing the sentence he told Smith that it was the most painful duty he ever had to perform; that they had fought side by side under the United States flag around the fortifications of the City of Mexico, but storming the Cassells of Carmel Hill was different from storming the castles around the city of Mexico, and as the jury had found him guilty it was his duty to pass sentence on him, which was about as follows: "The sentence of this court is; that you return to your home at Carmel Hill, and to remain peaceable, not leaving your home more than seven days in the week, also that you abstain from intoxicating drinks, not taking more than a drink three times a day and not over a pint each time, or pay a fine of fifty cents.

When in 1876 the Hampton campaign was launched to redeem South Carolina's white supremacy, Mackey changed sides in politics, joining the Democratic party, donned a red shirt, which he wore continuously, and made vigorous stump speeches all over the upper portion of South Carolina in advocacy of Hampton and White Man's Government. Through these speeches he had considerable influence over the Negroes and Carpet-baggers. After Hampton was elected, the Democrats got in power, Mackey, as a reward for his services, was re-elected judge. After serving this term he was defeated by I. D. Witherspoon, of York, for the judgeship of the sixth circuit. He then opened an office in Chester for the practice of law, but this kind of a life was too monotonous for his temperament, and about this time a new party sprang up in South Carolina known as the Greenback Party. He left the Democratic party and joined this new party and ran for Congress in this district, stumping the whole district in advocacy of himself, but was defeated. On one occasion to illustrate his great political acumen: ~

He had staged a meeting at Wilksburg, west of Chester. Some of John Hemphill's friends, gathered a crowd and attended the meeting and demanded a division of time in the speaking. This proposition, Mackey reluctantly agreed to, if Hemphill would speak first. This Hemphill refused, as it was Mackey's meeting. Mackey finally agreed to speak first with the distinct understanding that each party would have all the time they wanted. Mackey mounted the platform about eleven o'clock. After he had spoken about an hour a hard shower commenced to falling, the crowd dispersed to some out-building for shelter from the rain. After the rain was over the crowd returned to the speaking stand. Mackey again led off and continued to speak until about four o'clock in the afternoon when the Hemphill men wanted to know when he would be through. He said it was a distinct understanding between Mr. Hemphill and himself that they should have all the time they wanted and he presumed he would finish, if not interrupted, by nine or ten o'clock. The consequence was that Hemphill's friends all left and Mackey won the day as to the speaking.

After his defeat for Congress he moved to Washington, opened a law office there, got into several escapades, and finally died there. He was in many respects a wonderful man, full of energy, cared little for money, was strictly temperate in his habits and chaste in his language, a wonderful conversationalist, and always attracted a crowd around him of eager listeners whether what he was saying was imaginary or the truth. There was good in him, and there were faults. Let us draw the mantle of charity over his faults, and let his good live.

November 12, 1925

Sketch of Judge John Hemphill, of Texas

Was a Native Of Chester County – One Of The Most Distinguished Men Ever Produced In This County.

John Hemphill was a son of Rev. John Hemphill, D.D., and Jeanette Linn. His father, Rev. Hemphill, came to America in the year 1783 and first settled in Philadelphia. He had two half-brothers, James and Nathan, who had come to America previous to the Revolutionary War, Nathan settling in one of the Northern states; James coming to Chester county (then district) S. C. Both of these brothers joined the Whig army. Nathan was killed at the battle of Brandywine on the 11th of September, 1777. James was in the fighting in and around Chester county and upper South Carolina under Lacy, McLure and others, and was cited for conspicuous bravery at the defeat of Capt. Christian Huck, on the 12th of July, 1780, at Williamson's or Brattonville, York county. John only remained a short time in Philadelphia, coming to Chester, S. C., to live with his brother, James. After coming here he decided to study for the ministry. Consequently, attended a classical school taught by a Mr. Warnock near Richburg, then to a school taught by Rev. Joseph Alexander, D.D. From there to Dickinson College, Pa., where he graduated on May 3, 1702. He studied theology and was licensed to preach in 1794. Having received a call to Hopewell A. R. P. church in Chester county, S. C., he accepted it. In the meantime he had married Jane Linn, a daughter of Rev. Matthew Linn, and soon after coming to Hopewell he bought a home about half a mile south of the church. Here the subject of this sketch, Judge John Hemphill, was born on the 18th of December, 1803.

In early boyhood he attended a school at Hopewell church taught by James Young. Of Mr. Young we know very little. He made his home at the Rev. Jno. Hemphill's and taught school all his life. One peculiarity about his school was he commenced the first Monday in January, and ended the day preceding Christmas. He taught every day of the week, and the only holidays were the Saturdays before communion at Hopewell church and the Fourth of July. Under his instruction young Hemphill was well grounded in the primary principles of education. After finishing at this school he attended a classical school, located about three miles east of Pleasant Grove Presbyterian church. This school was taught by James Orr, an Irishman who came to America about 1800. He had taught in Ireland before coming to this country, and was considered a profound scholar. Under his tutelage John Hemphill was prepared for college. After finishing at this school he taught one year and then entered the junior class of Jefferson College of Pennsylvania in the summer of 1823, from which he graduated two years later with second honor of his class.

Returning to South Carolina after graduating, he taught a classical school for two years at Long Cane, Abbeville District and also one year in the Cedar Creek section of Richland district, about twelve miles north of Columbia.

Having decided to enter the profession of law he entered in 1829, the office of D. J. McCord, of Columbia, to prepare himself for his chosen profession, and in November of the same year was admitted to the practice in the Court of Common Pleas. He opened an office in Sumter in the district of Sumter. About one year later he was admitted to the practice in the Courts of South Carolina.

A short time after he began the practice of law, the Seminole Indians began to commit depredations in Florida. To quiet them the President of the United States called for volunteers. John Hemphill volunteered in a company made up in Columbia and was elected a Lieutenant. While this company was not engaged in any battle, yet they suffered greatly from exposure and climatic conditions. On their return and disbandment, he resumed the practice of law in Sumter, where he continued until the spring of 1838, when he decided to go West, which he did and located at Washington in the Republic of Texas, and was licensed to practice law by Judge Williamson of that district, on September, 11, 1838.

The courts of the Republic at this time consisted of a chief justice and several district justices, elected by both houses of Congress, for four years. In January, 1840, John Hemphill was elected judge for the 4th district, and thereby became a member of the Supreme Court by virtue of his election. In December of the same year the then Chief Justice resigned, and Judge Hemphill was elected to the Chief Justiceship.

In 1845 the Republic of Texas became a component part of the United States by annexation. This necessitated certain changes in her constitution and form of government. Therefore, a convention of the people was called by the governor. Judge Hemphill was elected a delegate from Washington county, and in its debates soon took a high stand. He was chairman of the Judiciary committee, and in this capacity formulated the principles of the organic law of the State that still exist.

The new constitution made many changes in the organic law. The supreme court was to consist of a Chief Justice and two Associate Judges to be appointed by the governor. As soon as the State government was formed under the Constitution, the Governor appointed Judge John Hemphill Chief Justice. Four years later the Constitution was amended making the office of all judges elective. Judge Hemphill was re-elected Chief Justice for six years, and again in 1856. In 1858 he was elected to succeed Gov. Sam Houston in the Senate of the United States. On December, 1859, he resigned as Chief Justice and took his seat in the Senate, thus having held the Chief Justiceship of Texas as a Republic and Texas a State for eighteen consecutive years. A little over a year after he took his seat in the United States Senate, Texas withdrew from the Union. He immediately resigned and returned home. He was soon thereafter elected one of the delegates from the State to Montgomery, Ala., to organize the provisional government of the Southern Confederacy. When the government was removed to Richmond, Va., he took his seat in the Senate of the Southern Confederacy, where he died on January 7, 1862. His body was taken back to Texas and given a State funeral, after which it was laid to rest in the public cemetery at Austin along by the side of other distinguished dead of Texas. His political life was too short to develop into fame. He will go down in history as judge, jurist, and scholar.

Judge Hemphill was never married. Many of his relatives reside in South Carolina. Among those that rose to some prominence were two brothers, Rev. W. R. Hemphill, D. D., professor in Erskine College, and Hon. James Hemphill, who served Chester county in both houses of the Legislature of South Carolina; nephews, Rev. W. Moffatt Grier, D. D., for several years President of Erskine College; Rev. Charles R. Hemphill, D. D.,

President of Presbyterian Theological Seminary at Louisville, Ky., J. C. Hemphill, former editor of the Charleston News and Courier, and Hon. J. J. Hemphill for ten years a representative in the lower house of Congress from the fifth district of South Carolina.

S. B. Lathan.
Chester, S. C., May 20, 1927.

Fourth of July at Caldwell's in 1852

(By S. B. Lathan)

Prior to the Civil War the Fourth of July was a notable day in this section of the State, as many of the older citizens were either sons or grandsons of those who fought at Fishing Creek, Fish Dam and King's Mountain to gain the independence of the United States, and the fire of their patriotism was kept alive on the altar of liberty.

This day was always looked forward to with great interest, both by the old and young, and was observed as a national holiday and usually there would be a big picnic or barbecue at some prominent place in the county and about sunrise the exercises were opened by firing a cannon, which continued intermittently during the day until late in the afternoon.

The first one I attended, or I can now recall, was at Caldwell's crossroad, where Jas. M. Caldwell now resides. This was about seventy-seven years ago. As I recall the program of the day was as follows: The militia of the county, consisting of two regiments, gave a drill. This took place about eleven o'clock and each captain formed his company and marched to a nearby old field, where they formed in regiment order. When so formed, the colonel and his staff rode up and took command, and after putting the men through several military evolutions, they were then formed in line and the colonel, with his staff, inspected them by riding down in front of the men at present arms and then back in the rear and up to the center, where he made a short speech congratulating the men on their fine appearance and efficiency and dismissed the parade.

The privates did not wear uniforms, but were dressed according to their own comfort, some in shirt sleeves and some wore "store clothes." All carried guns, some squirrel rifles and some long single barrel shot guns, with flint and steel lock. The captains wore blue frock coats with white pants, also cocked hats with large white feather in the side and swords and belts. They had epaulets on each shoulder of their coats. The lieutenant's uniform was the same except they wore only one epaulet on the right shoulder of the coat. The field officer was the same as the captain, except they wore boots. On the outside of their pants – the legs extending to the knee, and a large red sash under the sword belt and buckskin gloves extending up to the elbow.

After the muster dinner was served picnic style on a long table in a grove nearby, which was well prepared and plenty for all. After dinner most of the crowd gathered around a stand for the speaking – Hon. W. W. Boyce, Congressman from this district "oratoried" for an hour – praising South Carolina for what her men did in the Revolution and wound up by cussing out the Yankees for wanting to free the Negroes. Some other lesser lights, candidates for office, spoke of their fitness for the office they sought and how they loved the dear people, etc. About 4:00 o'clock in the afternoon the crowd began to disperse for home. This was the time the average young boy looked forward to as it was the time to pull off the fights for this particular time. I only remember two. The casus belli of one of them was a short time before. A sister of Mr. Mc. had eloped with and married Mr. R. and some busy body had told Mr. R. that Mr. Mc. said he was going to whip him the first time he saw him, and this being the first time they met Mr. R. tackled Mr. Mc. if he said so, and he neither denied or owned up. They stripped off coats, a ring formed, both stepped in and the slugging began, each party hollowing for his friend, after they had beaten each other to almost blood pulp, friends parted them, it was a draw. After they shook hands and made friends Mr. Mc. denied he had said what was imputed to him and said that if he had denied it before the fight Mr. R. might have thought he did so through fear.

Another fight was the result of imbibing too much "John Barleycorn" which was plenteous on the ground. This was between a farmer and an Irishman. After a few blows the Irishman was knocked down and his antagonist jumped on him and began choking him when the Irishman called out, "Take him off me, I don't want to hurt him." Others of like nature occurred.

On all these occasions no weapons of any description were used and no one was ever seriously hurt.

That was a memorable day in my early life. And emotions that were aroused in my breast when I viewed the colonel of that militia regiment and his staff, all rigged up in their gaudy uniforms and prancing steeds, review that gallant body of men. I saw reviews in the Confederate army by major generals, but none of them was equal to this.

I should have said at the outset that the meeting was opened with prayer and after prayer the reading of the Declaration of Independence by a young man, afterwards Dr. Douglas.

These celebrations were held yearly in the county, but in different localities, some times at Rich Hill cross road, now Richburg; Carmel Hill, Blackstock, Baton Rouge and other places.

The next one I attended was at Blackstock in 1855. About the same exercises were gone through with as at Caldwell's, except there was no cannon firing. The speaking of all was along the lines of gaining the independence of the United States. A Mr. Dawkins made the principal address. He was Solicitor of the Sixth circuit at this time.

The military feature was more elaborate, as there were several companies of Calvary besides the infantry. After the speaking and dinner the calvary, or at least a part of them, pulled off a tournament. This was the first and only one I ever witnessed, and had many thrills in connection.

Men with long whips were stationed along the course, and as the knights passed would lash the horses, making it difficult for the riders to stick to the saddle, or get many of the rings. It was considered disgraceful for a knight to be thrown from his horse. After the game was over the successful knight chose a young lady to be queen. The successful knight was a Mr. Lemon, and he chose a Miss Arnett for queen and the coronation was carried out after the style, "When knighthood was in bloom."

The last of these celebrations was pulled off at Pleasant Grove Presbyterian church, six miles southeast of Chester, in 1860.

Civil War Veteran Tells Story of First Submarine and First Torpedo Attack

"Cigar Boats and "Fish Boats" Were Constructed by the Confederates and Were Tried Out Against the Enemy in the Harbor of Charleston, S. C. – Samuel B. Lathan, Authority on Confederate History, Relates Historical Event.

By Sam W. Kluttz.

Samuel B. Lathan, of Chester, S. C., Confederate veteran, and one of the best known authorities on Confederate war history in the Carolinas, in an interview, recently brought to light some notable historical data about the first torpedo boats ever used in the history of this nation.

The first torpedo boat ever used in war, Mr. Lathan states, was christened the "Cigar Boat," which was built this latter part of 1863 by the Southern Confederacy, and brought into service against that historic battleship "Ironsides." It is indeed interesting, he says, to see the high class and honorable manner of attack carried on by the southerners as compared to the dishonorable tactics adopted by the German submarines in the world war.

Mr. Lathan likewise remarked that many folk may not know it, but the torpedo was an invention of Benjamin Franklin.

The "Fish Boat" followed the "Cigar Boat."

Historical Event.

Mr. Lathan's full interview, which is a most valuable contribution to southern history, is as follows:

"After the state of South Carolina passed the ordinance of secession withdrawing from the Union, Major Anderson, in command of the United States troops, then stationed at Fort Moultrie, on Sullivan's Island, immediately transferred his troops, consisting of about 85 officers and men, to Fort Sumter. On January 9, 1861, the United States government at Washington endeavored to send troops and provisions to him by the merchant steamer, "Star of the West," which was fired on by South Carolina troops then in possession of Fort Moultrie and forts on Morris Island, preventing her from accomplishing this end. Major Anderson being almost destitute of rations, appealed to the United States government, stating that without relief he could not hold out much longer. President Lincoln ordered the war department to send supplies and troops immediately to him, where-upon Jefferson Davis, president of the Confederacy, ordered General Beauregard to attack and capture Fort Sumter at once, which he did on April 12, and Major Anderson surrendered April 16, 1961.

Blockade of Port.

"The United States government then immediately sent a fleet of armed vessels to blockade the port of Charleston. Thus communication with the outside world by water was cut off. This fleet was stationed just outside the bar and completely cut off all vessels coming in with any kind of products of merchandise, except occasionally small vessels running past the fleet. This fleet a few times attacked the forts around the harbor, but with little or no effect. After some time the idea was conceived by some naval experts of destroying the blockaders by means of submarine torpedo boats. The first of these torpedo boats was built in the latter part of 1863. It was about 30 feet in length, 6 feet deep, and about 5 feet wide, called the "Cigar Boat." It tapered from the center to a point at each end, and had a tonnage of about 7,000 pounds. Its propelling force consisted of an eight-horsepower engine, and used anthracite coal for fuel.

"This engine was linked up to a shaft leading to the stern and attached to a propeller at its rear. At the prow was an iron bowsprit about 10 feet long and at its end a torpedo was fastened. When afloat about 14 feet of its length and 14 inches of its depth was above the water line. In the center there was a manhole through which the crew entered. When thus completed it came down Ashley river to one of the wharfs in Charleston. With Lieutenant Glassnell, a native of Virginia, and formerly an officer in the United States navy, with a crew of two men, one a pilot and the other an engineer. On the night of October 6, they loosed from the wharf and slowly moved towards the blockading fleet. The only armament they had was a torpedo fastened to the bowsprit in front, and a shotgun that the lieutenant took aboard. When they asked him what he was going to do with the shotgun he said, "attack the enemy."

Terrific Explosion.

"They moved down the channel at about six miles per hour, the night being very dark and cloudy. When they got within 50 yards of the battleship 'Ironsides,' one of the most powerful vessels of the United States navy, the lieutenant hailed the 'ship ahoy,' and when he received the answer, 'where away.' he said, 'I have come to attack you," and fired his shotgun at them, stopped the engine of his boat, lowered the torpedo and struck the Ironsides below the water line.

"The explosion of the torpedo threw tons of water over the gun railing of the ship, and falling back in the torpedo boat put out its fire. Lieutenant Glassnell and his pilot jumped overboard to escape the shots that were being fired by the marines who were assembled on the deck of the Ironsides. Glassnell cried for help. The marines ceased firing and sent a small boat and rescued him. The pilot swam back to the Cigar Boat, climbed in and he and the engineer baled her out, rekindled the fire and got her back to Charleston. Glassnell was taken to a northern prison. His health broke down and he died there. This was only a partial success. The Ironsides was damaged to such an extent that it had to be taken north and repaired.

"The next attempt was made in February 17, 1864, when another officer constructed another submarine boat called "The Fish Boat." This was 30 feet long, 6 feet wide and 4 feet 8 inches in the beam, and made of boiler iron. It tapered from the center to each end in a wedge shape about 12 feet from the prow on each side, with fins about seven inches wide, three-eighths of an inch thick, and four feet long, fastened to the shaft which passed in to the inside through a water tight fitting to a crank which was operated by man-power. By moving these cranks you could move the boat forward or backward, up or down. In the rear of it was a propeller which was also fastened to an air tight shaft and was worked by hand power.

Dived Under Vessel.

"On the bowsprit was an iron rod about 12 feet long, to it fastened a 150 pound torpedo, and as this boat had to be kept on an even keel, a ballast sufficient in weight to counteract the weight of the torpedo was kept in the stern. About 10 feet from the center on either end was two manholes. These were covered with very thick glass in an iron frame which fastened in the inside and made the boat waterproof. Between these two manholes was an opening into which was inserted two flexible tubes so that when the boat was in two feet of the surface, a valve could be opened and fresh air let in and the foul air driven out."

"The first crew that entered this boat consisted of eight men. They came down the Ashley River, dived under a vessel lying in the river and came upon the other side. After repeating this several times they went to the wharf, and for some reason the lieutenant in command and his chief went ashore. The remaining men, although not familiar with the working of the boat, pulled out, dived under the same ship and never came up any more. About three weeks afterwards, the boat was found and raised, the dead taken out and the boat disinfected.

"Another crew was secured and on boarding her at the wharf she sank. The Lieutenant and engineer managed to get out. She was again raised, and another crew of six men volunteered to go in it. After practicing diving in the harbor, they moved off to Mt. Pleasant wharf on 16th of February. On the 17th about sundown they pulled out from the wharf and headed towards the blockading fleet. The night was gloomy and overcast with clouds. Terrible cannonading was going on around the harbor. When they arrived at the fleet, the boat attacked the United States war vessel USS Housatanic, and nothing was heard of her until the next morning, when the heavy fog cleared about 9 o'clock, the Housatanic was discovered sunk and her men clinging to her riggings. What became of the "Fish Boat" was never definitely known at the time. It was generally thought that when the torpedo struck the Housatonic and exploded the hole in the side of the ship was so great, and the inrush of the water so heavy, that the "Fish Boat" was drawn in and went down with her."

This was the first time that any submarine boat had ever been used, and possibly the younger set may not know it, but the torpedo was an invention of Benjamin Franklin. Four years later to a day, Major Anderson, now a Major General, hoisted the same flag over Fort Sumter that he tore down when he surrendered the fort to the South Carolina troops."

H. L. Hunley, Submarine

The H. L .Hunley was a Confederate submarine built in Mobile, Alabama in 1863 and was originally calld the "fish boat" or "torpedo boat." It sank twice during training missions in Charleston, SC killing a total of 13 crew members, including the inventor Horace Hunley himself who was aboard in 1863. The "Hunley" was the first combat submarine to sink an enemy warship.

**S. Robert Lathan, author

McConnellsville

**Recollections of Noted York County Neighborhood.
Early a Business and Social Center
First Settlers Sold Their Cotton and Did Their Business in Columbia – Building of the Railroad – First Business Houses – Ancedotes of Revs. Lowry Wilson and Henry R. Dickson – The First Physicians.**

By S. B. Lathan.

About half way between Chester and Yorkville, or to be more accurate, twelve miles north of Chester and ten miles south of Yorkville on the Carolina and North-Western railroad, the prosperous and progressive village of McConnellsville is located. It got its name from Reuben McConnell, the father of the late Capt. John D. McConnell, who lived about two hundred yards south of the present station. I think the house is still standing, surrounded by some large oaks.

The residents of this section of York county in the early part of the last century, were to a great extent the ancestors of the present citizenship, viz.: The Loves, McConnells, Moores, Ashes, Lindsays, McKnights, Burrises, McCleaves. The lands were thought to be better suited to growing the cereals than cotton, consequently, a great deal of wheat and corn was raised, and on all the creeks were located good mills on which the wheat and corn was ground and, the planter could always get a ready market and a good price for his flour and corn meal in the surrounding towns. What cotton was grown had to be hauled to Columbia or Charleston to sell, there being no railroad facilities, made the marketing process a slow and uncertain one. It would take not less than five days for a wagon loaded with cotton to make the trip to Columbia and back to McConnellsville and, as the roads were always bad in the fall from constant and much use and, very little work done on them. About four bales was a load for a four-horse team. Generally from two to six farmers would make these trips together. They would try to get near Columbia and go into camp on the second night, drive into the city early next morning, sell their cotton, buy their groceries, which generally consisted of salt, sugar, coffee and molasses, go out of the city and camp for the night.

In one of these cotton caravans made up of some of the farmers from around McConnellsville, was a Mr. Burris and a Mr. McKnight. After the crowd had sold their cotton in the morning, purchased their groceries and, were moving out of the city, late in the evening, the news came by mail from Charleston that the market was up considerable. That night while Burris was preparing supper, Mr. McKnight was figuring how much he had lost by not waiting until evening to sell. Mr. Burris turned to him and waving the stick he was chunking the fire with, exclaimed that the price they sold for was "God's plenty for the cotton." After this Ned Burris's "Plenty" was a common expression around McConnellsville and vicinity.

When the railroad was surveyed from Columbia, S. C., to Charlotte, N. C., the business men of Yorkville were anxious to have it built through Yorkville and thence to Ebenezer and thence to Charlotte, Rock Hill was not then on the map, but, for some reason the Railroad authorities selected the present location. The citizens of Yorkville were determined not to be outdone and, with the co-operation of those living between there and Chester, decided to build a branch road to connect at Chester. After the proposition had been fairly discussed among the town people and country people at the courthouse, and I suppose at the country churches before service and during recess, it was determined to call a mass meeting at the courthouse and perfect an organization, get subscriptions to the capital stock etc. When the day arrived a large crowd had assembled, many speakers were on hand to show the great advantages that would accrue to the people along the line through which the road would pass, enthusiasm was at fever heat, the crowd in imagination could see the smoke and hear the whistle of the iron horse. In the crowd was an Irishman who lived near McConnellsville, who had a regular engagement to furnish a customer in Yorkville, three pounds of butter every week and, this was the day for his delivery of the butter. One of the speakers knowing this fact referred to it in his speech to show the advantage it would be to his friend that he could ship his butter by the train and save so much time. This son of Erin thought he was poking fun at him and exclaimed from the crowd what he was lugging in the wee bucket of butter for, that he made his living by honest toil and asked no favor from either him or his railroad and if he referred to him again he would mash his face so his "mither" would not recognize him from Jimmy O'Rourke's bull pup." Sufficient amount of stock was subscribed, an organization was perfected with the election of Col. Wm. Wright as president, a charter obtained and the road built. When completed the authorities located a station here for the receiving and discharging both freight and passengers, also, had a tank to get water and a wood yard. They gave to the station the name McConnellsville in honor of Reuben McConnell, who lived here as before mentioned.

Shortly afterward Mr. J. P. Moore, then clerking for a mercantile firm in Yorkville, formed a co-partnership with Mr. Hugh Burris and opened a business under the style of Moore & Burris. They built a storeroom in which to do business near the present store of J. P. Williams & Co., and did a lucrative business, mostly in dry goods and millinery, and as the ladies of this community were noted for dressing up to the height of the fashion and, the men for paying their bills, Moore & Burris had a soft snap in making money.

The Civil War soon broke out, the ports and all outside means of getting goods cut off, merchandising from 1862 to 1866 was a lost art. The people used parched rye for coffee, sorghum molasses for sweetening and, the ladies had to fall back to the styles of colonial days after their supply of store clothes were worn out and wear homespun and, the men did likewise, so Moore & Burris had to close up shop because they could not get any goods to sell. Mr. Moore told me the firm collected all their outstanding claims in Confederate money, invested most of it in Confederate bonds and, as a result the firm lost practically everything they owned.

Soon after they commenced business the U. S. government established a post office here which was located in the storeroom of Moore & Burris. I think Mr. J. P. Moore was the postmaster and continued to hold his office under the U. S. and Confederate government until the surrender, when the office was discontinued on account of no man in the community who could take the ironclad oath which required all persons taking office under the United States to swear that they never gave aid either directly or indirectly to the Confederate states. People from this community got their mail from Guthriesville. Miss Jane Guthries was the postmistress there in 1872.

Mr. A. F. Lindsay, who was a clerk for Moore & Hemphill was appointed postmaster, the oath being modified so he could take it.

After the war Mr. J. P. Moore and Samuel Hemphill formed a partnership and commercial business in the old stand of Moore & Burris. Their business was on a small scale at first but gradually increased until they had a very fair business. In 1872 Mr. E. N. Crawford built a store room just across the railroad opposite Moore & Hemphill and he, with Mr. A. F. Lindsay opened a store selling practically everything kept in a country store.

Mr. A. F. Lindsay, the postmaster, moved the post office from the Moore & Hemphill store to the store of Crawford & Lindsay. Sometime after Moore & Hemphill sold out their business to J. O. Moore and F. D. Williams. Mr. E. N. Crawford about this time built a shop in which he conducted a general repair work on wagons, buggies, horse-shoeing, etc. The place now commenced to take on new life, residences were erected and business began to expand.

Dr. W. M. Love and H. E. McConnell opened up offices and did the practice of community with McConnellsville as headquarters.

In 1870 I was chosen teacher for the McConnellsville school. At that time there were only three houses where the village now stands, viz: The residences of Capt. Jno. D. McConnell and J. P. Moore and the store room of Moore & Hemphill. The school building was located about a quarter of a mile east of the station and was a very crude affair, both as to its construction and equipment and, entirely out of keeping with the financial conditions of the patrons. However, I got along nicely as I had the full cooperation of the patrons and the attention of the pupils. The patrons of this school lived within a radius of two miles with McConnellsville as a center. They were above the average in intelligence and piety, were well fixed financially and taught their children to be obedient and to read the Bible and observe the Sabbath day. They might have been divided into four families, viz: Ashes, Loves, McConnells, and Burris, and if any one did not have one of these names he or she was kin to some one of them. They were all distinctly Presbyterians in their religion. A few attended Zion now Lowryville Presbyterian church. Others Old Olivet, which stood about three miles west of McConnellsville and, whose membership was made up of New School Presbyterians, Associate Reformed Presbyterians and Old School Presbyterians. When the churches in York county of the New School Presbyterian were absorbed by Bethel Presbytery, Olivet was taken under the care of Bethel Presbytery and the Associate Reformed Presbyterians vacated the field. Bethesda was the Drumtrochity of this section and the second Sabbath in May and September being the dates of Spring and Fall communion, were the "big days" religiously speaking. Vast crowds came from all sections of the country. These people were noted for their sociability; they were all friends, no neighborhood broils but all on good terms with each other. Rev. W. W. Ratchford preached for the Olivet people twice a month. He lived at Howe place where Mr. Frank Ashe now lives. And, by the way, at this place at one time a certain man ran a liquor shop, sold some groceries and also was a kind of jack-leg tailor. This was before the railroad was built. I think Mr. Ratchford got $150.00 per year for his service. Rev. J. Lowry Wilson was chosen pastor of Bethesda and Zion in 1863 and took charge early 1870. He was fresh from the Seminary, had always lived in town and had much to learn of country life. He was born in Allahabad, India, and when twelve years old was sent to the United States to be educated. Soon after graduating the Civil War commenced, he entered the Confederate States army as Lieutenant and lost a leg in Virginia. After the war he taught school two years at Bethesda then went to the Theological Seminary at Columbia and came back to Bethesda as pastor three-fourths of his time and Zion one-fourth. He boarded at Dr. Robert L. Love's where it was also my good fortune to board. He was a hard student and wrote in full all his sermons and generally sticking close to his manuscript in delivery. He was held in high esteem by the whole community, was a great punster, but had much to learn of country life, — as an illustration, in visiting among his congregation it always worried him for them to prepare a big dinner on his account. One evening he told me he had worked out a plan to overcome it and, it was this, - to find out the dinner hour of the family he was to visit and manage to drop in just as they were ready to sit down or had already been seated at dinner and, they would not have time to prepare anything extra. I told him that would put them to more trouble than if he went earlier, as none of them would set the preacher down to dinner without something extra. He was a good conversationalist and enjoyed good company. Rev. Henry Dixon, pastor of the Presbyterian church at Yorkville, and he were warm friends, and Mr. Dixon would frequently spend Mondays with him talking over church matters, etc. He would come down on the train in the morning and return in the afternoon.

Mrs. Love kept a Negro girl about 14 or 15 years old who Mr. Wilson had nicknamed "Folly" because she always had a broad grin on her face, on one of these visits she sent this Negro with a horse to the station for Mr. Dixon to ride. When he got off the train, and Mr. J. P. Moore showed him his conveyance, the girl insisted on riding behind him to the strenuous objection of Mr. Moore, when the couple got near Dr. Love's "Folly" struck the grit and walked. That evening when Mrs. Love and Mr. Wilson heard of it they were worried not knowing what Mr. Dixon thought of it. When the old cook learned it she took "Folly" in hand and, I dare say "Folly" never forgot what happened. Mr. Wilson never married, he demitted his charge then went to the Abbeville Presbyterian church and died sometime ago.

Dr. R. L. Love with whom I boarded was the only practicing physician in this community, consequently his practice was very extensive. He always rode horseback and carried the proverbial saddle bags from which he dispensed his medicines. His practice was almost entirely therapeutical, occasionally he would be called on to perform a minor operation, such as pulling a tooth or setting a broken limb for some boy who had fallen out of a tree while gathering muscadines or scalybarks in the Fall of the year. The people were not up on sanitation then as now and, there was a great deal of chills and malaria in this section during the fall months which kept him on the go all the time and, if he had been a good collector as he was a practitioner he would have left his children a fortune. There was a Mr. Halsel living at Dr. Love's, who was addicted to the opium habit, on one occasion he took an overdose and Dr. Love made two Negroes take hold of his arms and walk him and, had "Willie," as Dr. W. M. was then called, pull up Halsel's pants to knees and whip his bare legs. It was amusing to see how Halsel would squirm and kick as Willie applied the switch and laugh. After an hour or two of this exercise Halsel got all right, his legs rather sore from the effects of the switch applied by Willie, who for sometime had only a distant relationship with Halsel.

During the reconstruction and immediately after, McConnellsville was one of the places in York county where the Negroes and scalawags held their big political powwows. On these occasions the Negroes from all the surrounding neighborhood would assemble, a brass band was always on hand as it created more enthusiasm in the average country person than all their speech making, therefore, it had a very prominent part in the program and did much "tooting." They had only one tune and they played it for all it was worth. During the speaking Capt. Jim Williams had his company of militia on hand and after the meeting closed Capt. Jim gave an exhibition drill by his company, which consisted of double-quicking his men for about an hour over an old field near the station. Erstwhile Capt. Jim came to grief. On the night of the first Monday in March, 1871, Dr. Love and I had been out west of McConnellsville for a fox chase and when returning about a half mile from McConnellsville, we were halted and demanded to know who we were and where going, after a short delay we were ordered to follow them and when we got to the station we discovered that they were Ku Klux as we had suspected. They made the Negro pumper get up behind one of the men but Mr. J. P. Moore interceded for him and they let him go. They inquired about several Negroes in the vicinity but finally the leader said they must hurry on as they wanted Williams and could take no chances. The next morning Jim Williams was found hanging to a limb of a pine tree near the Scott Wilson place. This event created a great commotion among the Negroes of the neighborhood, several left the country and, the men who remained slept at night in the woods for sometime fearing a return of the Klan. It was not an unusual thing to see between sundown and dark Negroes with blankets on their shoulders making for the woods to spend the night. The Negro militia company automatically disbanded with the hanging of Williams. The Klan that did the hanging was known as the "Briar patch Klan" and was made up from the Sharon section of the county. In a patch of woods not far from where Jim Williams was hung, is a marble slab marking the grave of the Black servant of Col. Wm. Bratton of revolutionary fame and, the slab was placed at his grave by Col. Bratton to commemorate his faithfulness to his master during the Revolutionary war, a peculiar coincidence.

Of all the patrons of the school during the time I taught there, not one is living today. Also a great many of the pupils have passed to the Great Beyond. Those that are living are the old people of the community, and in closing this article I want to say to them, May they be spared the sharp passions of a unguarded moment, may they never forget that poverty and riches are spirit and, although age and infirmity overtake them, and they come not within sight of the castle of their dreams, teach them to be thankful for life and times olden memories that are good and sweet and may the evening's twilight be gentle still.

Godfather of York

Alexander Love Was Head of First Colony

Settled on Fishing Creek in 1763

Progenitors of the Loves and Moores of the Guthriesville and McConnellsville Neighborhoods – Important Historical Data as to York County.

By Sam B. Lathan.

Among the emigrants who came from Pennsylvania and settled in the upper portion of South Carolina prior to the Revolutionary war was an Alexander Love, and family. These emigrants generally came in colonies and where they located was known as such and such a settlement. Alexander Love and the parties who came with him settled on Fishing Creek not far from Yorkville, and south of where the Marion and Kingville branch of the Southern railway crosses it. This was known as the upper Fishing Creek settlement, Craven county, North Carolina. I would state here by way of parenthesis that the separation of North Carolina and South Carolina was officially ordered in 1729, but it was not effected until 1732. The dividing line was run in 1735 and then very incorrectly, which caused considerable trouble among those living on the line. In 1763 the king ordered a resurvey made of the dividing line and this resurvey gave South Carolina a large tract of territory which was called "The New Acquisition," so this section was first Craven county, North Carolina, afterwards Craven county, South Carolina, then "The New Acquisition," and now York county, South Carolina.

Alexander Love married Margaret Moore. The Loves and the Moores were both of Scotch-Irish ancestry. The Loves were Presbyterians in religious faith and worship, and the Moores belonged to the sect known as Friends, or as designated by others, as Quakers. Alexander Love and Margaret Moore were married on the 6th of March 1743. The marriage caused a considerable commotion. This society of Friends, as the Quakers called themselves, did not permit of any of their members marrying out of their creed and, as a consequence Margaret was turned out of the society and forever disowned by them. The society also had one of her brothers up for trial for conniving at the marriage and suspended him for a time from the society. There was no objection by the Moore family to Alexander Love marrying Margaret. It was altogether a religious affair. After Love's marriage, he settled in York county, Pennsylvania, and lived there for some time. About 1763 he moved to the then Craven county, North Carolina, now York county, South Carolina, and soon became a very prominent and influential citizen in his new home. He was one of the fourteen members from the New Acquisition, to the Provincial congress of South Carolina which met in Charleston of that state on the first day of November 1775. This position was rather forced upon him as it would take him for sometime away from his home and, at considerable expense and inconvenience but he being a staunch Whig, was willing to undergo these inconveniences that his country might get from under the British yoke.

When York district was laid off, he being a member of the legislature succeeded in having it named York, after his old home county in Pennsylvania. He accumulated considerable property, both in lands and personal property, as shown by his will which is recorded in Craven county, N. C. He took an active part in all religious affairs and was a ruling elder in Bethesda Presbyterian church, of which he had been a member since coming to his new home. He reared a family of eleven children, five sons and six daughters. His eldest daughter, Rachel, married Francis Ross, who at the outbreak of the revolutionary war became an active partisan and continued so until his death. He enlisted and commanded a battalion of cavalry which served under Col. Hammond. On the morning of March 29th, 1779, they attacked a party of Tories and Cherokee Indians, near Rocky Point now in Aiken county, S. C. Major Ross was mortally wounded. He died on the 31st of March and was buried with military honors April 1st, near where the present town of Hamburg SC, is located.

Andrew, the second son of Alexander Love was a very active Whig and was among the first to take up arms in the cause of his country. He was wounded at King's Mountain and rose to the rank of colonel. Like all the Scotch-Irish, he was particularly severe on those who remained loyal to the British crown and were termed by their neighbors, Tories. His sister, Sarah, married one of these loyalists, and on one occasion he learned there was to be a meeting held by these Tories at his brother-in-law's house, located on Fishing Creek, on the plantation lately owned by Capt. Thomas Lowry, deceased. With a portion of his command he surrounded the house and ordered them to surrender. This they refused to do, Col. Love then notified them he would shoot the first man who came out. His sister unfortunately came to the door wearing a hat when one of his men shot and killed her. After the war he represented York district, S. C., several years in the legislature. He moved to Kentucky in 1805 and was found dead one day in his field with marks of violence on his body. His son Alexander Love, built the second residence in Yorkville.

Robert, another son, was a soldier in the Revolutionary War, and it is related that after the war that he was so anxious to see his affiance that he walked 72 miles in one day and a part of a night, and from this over exertion took down with a fever and died suddenly. His affiance, Margaret McDowell, afterwards married his brother William. They moved to Mississippi in 1806 where he died.

Two sons and two sons-in-law of Alexander Love rose to prominence in the Revolutionary War, taking active parts in fighting the British troops and suppressing the bands of Tories that infested the country. This is not strange, as no doubt they had heard around the home firesides of their parents the rehearsal of the cruelties inflected on their ancestors who were driven from Scotland and Ireland during the reign of Charles II and James II, and left to seek a home in the wilds of America where they might enjoy that civil and religious liberty they never could in their native land. These pilgrims taught their children to fear God, study the Bible, memorize the shorter catechism and hate tyrants and wherever they located they implanted these teachings. Alexander Love, himself, a ruling elder in Bethesda Presbyterian church, has continually had one of his lineal decendants on the eldership of this church until the present day. All the Loves, Moores, and Lindsays in and around McConnellsville and Guthriesville are his direct offspring.

Alexander Love died March 1784 and was buried in Bethesda cemetery adjoining the old church of that name, near the present village of Guthriesville, where he had been a ruling spirit from the time he settled in this section. His grave is marked by a marble slab which bears the following inscription: "Alexander Love died March 1784, aged 66 years, A lover of mankind, A friend to his country."

From Ancient Court House Records

(By Mrs. Jesse S. Carter)

The Packenham Legend.

(Mr. S. B. Lathan had the story many times from his father.)

The country store of the period handled large quantities of rum and other intoxicants and was for that reason the rendezvous of the thirsty.

This incident took place about 1817, at the country store of Daniel McMillin (commonly called Danny McMullin) in the upper end of Fairfield county, South Carolina.

One day a hard drinker named Jack —, having fallen into a drunken stupor, was put into an empty cask by some practical jokers, who headed the cask and painted upon its sides: "General Packenham – went away in high spirits, returned in low wines."

This choice bit of "foolery" after fifty or sixty years of re-telling resolved itself into the myth that General Packham's body, shipped in rum – for preservation – from New Orleans to Liverpool was by mistake reshipped to South Carolina in a consignment of liquors, and that when his body was discovered at the bottom of an emptied cask it was buried four or five miles from Blackstock.

The War of the 60's

Most Interesting Article by S. B. Lathan.

The Excitement That Prevailed In South Just Prior To The Outbreak Of The Struggle – The Contest Between Secessionists And Co-operationists – Chester's Five Companies That Went Out In 1861 – Lasted Four Years To The Day.

When the national Democratic convention met in Charleston, S. C., in April, 1860, the whole country was stirred up over the John Brown raid on Harper's Ferry for the avowed purpose of freeing the slaves in the slave states of the United States. Although Brown was tried, convicted and hung together with six of his company, nevertheless, feeling ran high and bitter between the South and North, as the excitement over this raid which had occurred only a few months before. The delegates to this convention from the slave States wanted a candidate from the South and the Northern delegates, wanted one from the North. After wrangling and filibustering for about a week or ten days the meeting broke up without getting together or making a nomination. The southern delegates afterward nominated John C. Breckenridge, of Kentucky, and the northern delegates nominated Stephen A. Douglass, of Illinois. The Republican or as it was called the Abolitionary party nominated Abraham Lincoln, of Illinois, and the old Whig party nominated John C. Bell, of Tennessee. As the Democrats ran two candidates as might have been expected the Republicans won out at the general election. All the different parties denounced the Brown raid in their platforms and made the usual buncombe of standing by the constitution.

There had been for sometime a class in South Carolina who favored secession – but never had much of a following in the up country, up to this time. The election of an avowed abolitionist for president – backed up by an abolitionist party aroused them to life and activity. The people were divided into three classes, viz: those favoring immediate secession single handed and alone; another class who wanted all the slave-holding states to act together and still another class who wanted to wait until Lincoln and his party committed some overt act against the slave states. These favoring immediate and separate secession were in the saddle, an organization known as minute men formed companies or lodges in nearly every county in the state, they claimed that their purpose and end was to take South Carolina out of the Union. It was composed mostly of young men and middle aged men. Their only regalia was a blue rosette worn on the side of their hat. The press of the country was full of controversies of these two factions, secession and co-operation were discussed pro and con at every gathering and cross road store in the county and at churches before and after service.

An amusing incident occurred in Chester county. A prominent citizen, a strong advocate of co-operation, wrote a series of articles for *The Chester Standard*, a weekly paper published in Chester. The articles advocating co-operation were signed "Co-operationist," and those advocating immediate secession, "Secessionist." These articles created different parties. He would always present the stronger arguments in favor of co-operation. His identity was never found out until after the State had seceded.

Mass meetings were held all over the county at which were prominent speakers. The most of these speakers hooted at the idea of war and said if war did come it would not last three months. Some even went so far as to assert they would drink all the blood that would be shed, that the Yankee would not fight. That one man from the South could whip four from any Yankee state. I must confess that in hearing so much of this kind of talk, I got to thinking that way myself and I believed that one soldier from South Carolina could put to flight three from any other state. I was convinced to the contrary a little later when it came to the actual show down.

When the legislature met, it authorized the governor to call a convention of the people through delegates at act upon this issue. The co-operationists realized they were defeated and that immediate secession would follow.

The convention was called to meet in Columbia on the 18th of December, 1860. The following were chosen without opposition from Chester county, viz.: Dr. Thos. Moore, John McKee, Richard Woods, and Quay Dunovant. The delegates met in Columbia but on account of the prevalence of smallpox in that city adjourned to Charleston, meeting in what was known as Secession Hall. On the 20th of December without a dissenting voice voted "That the Union now existing between South Carolina and other states under the name of the United State of America is hereby dissolved." The news was received with much demonstrations by the Secessionists, firing of cannon, bonfires, burning of Lincoln and other rank abolitionists in effigy. But some of the older and more conservative men viewed it in a more serious light. When I told my father that the ordinance of secession had been passed by the convention, after thinking a few moments he remarked "That is the death knell of slavery. There will be war and you and William make your arrangements to go."

I did not take his prediction very seriously as I had heard so much talk to the contrary. The convention authorized the governor to raise and equip a standing army of regulars to consist of one regiment of artillery, one of infantry and one battalion, also of infantry. R. H. Anderson, afterward Lieutenant General in the C. S. A. army, was appointed Colonel, R. S. Ripley, colonel of the artillery regiment and Maxcy Gregg to the command of the infantry battalion. On the 26th of December, 1860, Major Anderson transferred the U. S. garrison from Ft. Moultrie, Sullivan's Island, to Fort Sumter, which created some excitement in Charleston. Gov. Pickens was authorized and instructed by the legislature now in session to raise and equip ten regiments of volunteer infantry for service in South Carolina. Chester county's pro-rata was five companies which were raised without any trouble. These companies were as follows:

Chester Grays – Capt. O. Hardin.
Chester Blues – Capt. E. C. McLure.
Calhoun Guards – Capt. Walker.
Catawba Guards – Capt. Lafayette Strait.
Pickens Guards – Capt. Michael Moore.

These with five companies from Fairfield county composed the 6th S. C. Volunteers. The men elected all their officers from Colonel to Corporal. Jas. H. Rion was elected Colonel, E. Secrest, Lt. Colonel and T. W. Woodward, Major. These troops were being drilled every week. The harbor around Charleston was being strengthened by the erection of Fort Johnson on James Island and other fortifications on Morris Island and other points. These were garrisoned by the Washington artillery, and the Citadel Cadets, and other volunteers from different sections of the State. On the 9th of January, 1860, the President of the United States attempted to get relief to Major Anderson at Fort Sumter, both of men and provisions, by a merchant vessel, "The Star of the West," but the ship was fired on by the fortifications garrisoned with South Carolina volunteers. This event created considerable alarm throughout the State, and aroused the war spirit to fever heat. By the first of February six other southern states had withdrawn from the United States: Georgia, Florida, Alabama, Mississippi, Louisiana and Texas. On the 4th of February delegates from all these states except Texas met in Montgomery, Alabama, and organized a provisional government under the name of Confederate States of America. The delegates from Texas arrived a little later. These delegates elected Jefferson Davis, of Mississippi, president, and Alexander Stephens, of Georgia, vice president.

In South Carolina the leading topic of conversation was Fort Sumter, would Major Anderson voluntarily surrender it, or would he be starved out or would he be bombarded out? The facilities for getting news was confined mostly to the daily papers. Consequently every day when the trains arrived from Columbia crowds were out at the station enquiring what's the news from Charleston, "When will Fort Sumter be taken and etc.?"

The political atmosphere began to gradually cool down and look as if peaceable separation of the Southern states might be a possibility. However, when Abraham Lincoln, President-elect, delivered his inaugural on the 4th of March after induction into office all this view changed. In that address he used the following language.

"I have no purpose directly or indirectly to interfere with the institution of slavery in states where it exists. I believe I have no lawful right to do so, and I have no inclination to do so. I believe the union perpetual, and I will do my utmost to preserve, protect and defend it, and will use its power to retake the forts and other national property seized by the Confederacy."

The war cloud again began to loom up in the horizon. Major Anderson although scarce of provisions, still held Fort Sumter with no idea of surrender. The slogan "When will Fort Sumter be taken", was the current topic of inquiry on all sides. One day at Blackstock when the train arrived from Columbia, in the crowd was a very aggressive Minute Man, who rushed up to the Conductor, asking the news from Charleston, as this was his custom every day and the conductor getting tired of him said, "Fort Sumter will be attacked tomorrow and an extra train was following them picking up every Minute Man they could find. The man taking off his hat, jerked the rosette off and throwing it on the ground remarked, "I have a wife and two children to look after and am not going." The crowd yelled. After this he took a back seat.

Conditions at Fort Sumter were getting serious with the garrison. Their provisions were nearly exhausted. Major Anderson had made frequent appeals to Washington for help, and President Lincoln had ordered the War Department to supply him with both men and provisions as soon as possible. Jeff Davis, President of the Confederate States, to prevent these supplies reaching Major Anderson, ordered Gen. P. T. Beauregard, commanding the fortifications around Charleston, to attack and take Fort Sumter. This he proceeded to do and on the 8th of April the volunteer troops of the State were ordered to Charleston. On the morning of the 9th the Sixth Regiment entrained and was on the way. About sunrise April 12th the Confederate batteries opened on Ft. Sumter, after a formal demand of surrender was refused. After a continuous bombardment for 34 hours Fort Sumter surrendered. The U. S. flag was hauled down and the State flag of South Carolina was hoisted in its stead. Maj. Anderson asked and it was granted him to salute the flag before hauling it down.

Lincoln issued a proclamation on calling for seventy-five thousand volunteers to put down the rebellion. Virginia, North Carolina, Arkansas and Tennessee immediately withdrew from the United States and joined the Southern Confederacy, the capital of which was transferred to Richmond. The ten S. C. volunteer regiments re-enlisted as Confederate State troops – war was on – and lasted until April 9th, 1865 – four years to a day, when the 6th regiment entrained for Charleston. On the 13th of April, 1865, Major Anderson, now a Major General, hoisted the same flag over Ft. Sumter he had hauled down – exactly four years. This prediction of my father came true, we had war, and so William and I were in it till the finish, and the slaves of the South were emancipated.

S. B. Lathan.
Chester, S. C., Dec. 2, 1921.

THE SEVENTEENTH S. C. V.

Memory Sketch of Famous Fighting Unit.

FOUGHT THROUGH MANY CAMPAIGNS

Recruited Principally From York, Chester, Lancaster, Fairfield and Barnwell—Followed Fortunes of the Confederacy to Appomattox.

Written for The Yorkville Enquirer by S. B. Lathan of Chester, and one of the few survivors.

Installment I.

In writing the following sketch I will not attempt to give a complete history of the Seventeenth Regiment, S. C. V., C. S. A.; but the movement of the regiment from place to place—and the battles in which it was en-

.........this account is written as if SBL was with his 17th SC Regiment the entire duration. In the account of his personal War record noted in Section Two, he describes his assignments during the four year period. In this vivid description of daily life, he documents the movement of the regiment from the perspective of the enlisted man.

**S. Robert Lathan, Author

.......in the spring of 1907 I wrote and published in the *Chester Lantern* a series of articles concerning the movements of the regiment. The present sketch is a revision of the former, eliminating some things and adding others.

In getting up the former sketch my memory was refreshed by J. T. Marion and S. Kitchen, who kept diaries; also by Capt. W. H. Edwards, W. O. McKeown, H. White and possibly others. SBL

Written for the *Yorkville Enquirer* in 1923 by S. B. Lathan of Chester, and one of the few survivors.

The Seventeenth S. C. V.

Memory Sketch Of Famous Fighting Unit Fought Through Many Campaigns

Recruited principally from York, Chester, Lancaster, Fairfield and Barnwell—Followed Fortunes of the Confederacy to Appomattox.

Installment 1

In writing the following sketch I will not attempt to give a complete history of the Seventeenth Regiment, SCV.,C.S.A.; but the movement of the regiment from place to place- and the battles in which it was engaged from the organization at Camp Hampton, until it surrendered at Appomattox with the balance of General Lee's army.

About the first of November 1861 four companies from York District, commanded respectively by Captains W.H. Wilson, Jno. A. Witherspoon, Thos. Meacham and Lucian Saddler; of one company from Chester, Captain J. R. Culp, one company from Fairfield, Captain Preston Coleman, one company from Lancaster, Captain Caskey and one company from Chester and Fairfield, Captain James Beatty, assembled at Camp Hampton, near Columbia and organized into a battalion. They elected J. H. Means lieutenant colonel, F. W. McMaster major.

It was understood that as soon as we could get the required number of companies, Means was to be colonel and McMasters lieutenant colonel.

In a short time the necessary number of companies to complete the regiment joined us, when the two above named officers were promoted and Julius Mills, of Chester, was elected major. The letters of companies were as follows:

Company A, Captain Culp of Chester
Company B, Captain Coleman of Fairfield
Company C, Captain Witherspoon of York
Company D, Captain Beatty of Fairfield
Company E, Captain Meacham of York
Company F, Captain Wilson of York
Company G, Captain Sanders of Barnwell
Company H, Captain Rice of Barnwell
Company I, Captain Caskey of Lancaster
Company K, Captain Saddler of York

The companies of the regiment were mustered into service by General J. C. Preston of the Confederate War Department. The regiment, however, was mustered as State Troops, the men having volunteered for twelve months service to the State of South Carolina.

About the first of December, the regiment was sent to Charleston and went into camp on the south side of the Ashley river bridge. There the men were armed with old smooth bore muskets that had been changed from the old flint lock to percussion lock. Eight of the companies were armed with these antiquated guns: but the right and left companies A and E drew new English made Enfield rifles.

The uniforms of the companies were all different and were furnished by the communities in which the companies were enlisted. These were the only uniforms the men ever had. They were good clothes and lasted about a year. After they were worn out the men wore whatever kind and color of clothes they could get except black or blue.

We named this place " Camp Lee." General R. E. Lee was then in command of the defenses of South Carolina and the Georgia seacoast. While in this camp the measles broke out among the men resulting in many casualties in the regiment.

It was at this camp that Colonel Means first took command of the regiment. The lieutenant colonel having had charge of it up to this time. Dr. Wilson Wylie was commissioned surgeon and Robert H. Jordan assistant surgeon of the regiment. They were both of Chester county.

While we were at Camp Lee we drilled daily in company and battalion maneuvers, guard duty, and other camp duties.

On the first of February we were ordered to Wadmalaw Island. We broke camp on the morning of the 2nd taking up the line of march, crossed the Stono river at the ferry and camped for the night near the ferry where we crossed. The next morning, continuing the march about ten miles, we crossed a marsh or creek, which separates Johns and Wadmalaw Islands and arrived in the afternoon at Rockville, where we went into camp at the club house. While camped here, we did picket duty in both Johns and Wadmalaw Islands.

On the 12th of February, the regiment was moved to Johns Island and went into camp about five miles from Church Flats, at the Curtis house near a church. The regiment used the "Curtis" house as a field hospital while camped here. This camp was named "Camp Pillow". While stationed here we still did picket duty on Wadmalaw Island and Johns Island. Most of the time was employed in drilling, camp guard, and fatigue duty.

On the 12th of May, 1862 while the regiment was stationed at Camp Pillow on Johns Island it was reorganized for Confederate service. This was necessitated by an act passed by the Confederate congress known as the "Conscript Act ,"which required all male citizens between the ages of eighteen and forty-five to enlist in some organization, and also permitting those over and under the above ages to go home or join some other company if they so desired.

This made several changes among the men and officers of the regiment. Col. Means was re-elected, as was also Lieutenant Colonel McMaster. R.H. Means was elected Major instead of Julius Mills, James Conner was appointed adjutant, W.B.Metts commissary and Isaac Means quartermaster with Wm. Wylie surgeon.

The following changes occurred among the company officers:

Company A, Captain J. R. Culp re-elected
Company B, Captain Preston Coleman re-elected
Company C, Captain John A. Witherspoon re-elected
Company D, Captain James Beatty re-elected
Company E, Captain Meacham retired, Captain Holley of York was elected
Company F, Captain W. B. Wilson retired, Captain W. J. Avery was elected
Company G, Captain Sanders retired, Captain Wm Dickinson of Barnwell was elected
Company H, Captain Rice retired, Captain Ray of Barnwell was elected
Company I, Captain Caskey retired. Captain James Steele of Lancaster was elected
Company K, Captain Saddler retired, Captain E. A. Crawford of York was elected

I will not attempt to give the names of the lieutenants of the companies at this time as I would get mixed as to their rank. Some of their names, however, will figure in this narrative, some of them as captains and some in other positions.

Installment II

After the reorganization of the regiment we remained on Johns Island only a short time, as the weather was very hot and the water bad. Country fever commenced to break out among the men and this made the change necessary to the health of the regiment.

I would state here that we used well water entirely. These wells were secured by digging holes in the sand four or five feet deep and placing an empty flour barrel in them for a curbing. This would give us fairly good water for about a week, after which the wells would fill up and we would have to dig others.

We broke camp and moved out to the main land to a place called Rantowles on the Charleston and Savannah railroad. While stationed here we still did picket duty on Johns Island. After remaining here a short time the Yankees made a landing at Legareville on the island. Our regiment was ordered on the island and remained there several days.

On the march toward Legareville, a small body of the cavalry was retreating at full speed--being chased by a superior force of Yankee cavalry. A small squad of men who were in front passed the Seventeenth Regiment (some of the companies of which had fallen out of the road, some on the right and some on the left) and shouted:

"The Yanks are just behind us!" Our men construed this to mean that no more of our cavalry was in their rear. This was not the case, for there was another squad of our cavalry behind them. The regiment taking this to be Yanks- opened fire on them and wounded several.

The Yankee cavalry halted and went back, and before the regiment could march to Legareville, they had left the island.

There was an amusing incident when out cavalry was passing us --a member of company "D" had a perfect terror of a horse--and when the first squad was passing his eyes commenced to look like full moons; but when the second squad came into sight, he made a break down the road in the opposite direction at full speed, crying at the top of his voice, "Murder, murder." Seeing he was going to be overtaken, he jumped off a small bridge into the marsh and sank to his waist in the mud and water. Some of the men had to pull him out.

In the evening when we returned to camp from this march, about the time when the regiment had formed in line (which was done before breaking ranks) Captain Holley of York fell dead of heart failure. He never spoke or breathed after he struck the ground. He was a fine officer and educated Christian gentleman.

E. R. Mills, then became Captain of Company E.

We returned to Rantowles and while there James P. Hurst who was orderly sergeant of Company "H" was appointed chaplain of the regiment and served in that capacity until after the second battle of Manassas, when he retired.

Up to that time the Seventeenth Regiment had been without a chaplain; but not altogether without religious services. Captain Witherspoon held prayer meetings in his own company and a great many of the men of the other companies attended.

The regiment was next moved to a few miles further down the railroad towards Logansville. While we were at this camp, the Yankees made an attempt from Hilton Head to cut the railroad at Pocotaligo. We were hurried down there on cars; but when we arrived we found the enemy had been driven back by some of our cavalry.

We pursued them all night but only twice got in sight of them before they reached safety under cover of their breast works around Hilton Head. The regiment returned the next morning by the same route it had marched the previous night. We arrived in Pocataligo about four in the afternoon, boarded a train, which was waiting for us and got back to camp about sun down, pretty badly used up. We had marched all the night before and were hungry, sleepy, and tired.

At a another time three regiments of the brigade were thrown across the river to Johns Island after night and camped for an hour or two in Governor Aiken's Negro village. Soon, however, a courier came with orders for us to return. We learned afterwards that the Yankees had a strong force on the island and occupied a splendid position to withstand an attack, but we had no artillery and no way to take it with us. When we returned the tide was down and the boat could not get near the shore; the gang planks were sunk in the mud and many would miss the planks and get stuck knee deep in the nasty, slimy salt water slush.

But to compensate us for the loss of sleep, a hard march and getting stuck in the mud, Gen. N. G. Evans had sent down a barrel of whiskey, which was issued in water buckets with the cups to drink it out of. The men had a dandy time that night. I recollect hearing one of the captains singing that night to a crowd:

> *"Give him strong drink until he wink*
> *That's sinking in despair*
> *In liquor gude to fire his bluch*
> *When prest with grief and care*
> *Then let him house in deep enrouse*
> *In bumpers flowing Pre*
> *Till he forgets his loves and debts*
> *And minds his griefs no more."*

There were rumors about this time that the brigade was soon to be transferred to the trans-Mississippi department. Other rumors had us going to the army of Tennessee and still others to Virginia.

The matter was definitely settled when at dress parade on the evening of the 19th of July, the Seventeenth Regiment received orders to prepare rations and get ready to move to Richmond, VA on the 21st.

This was glad news to most of us as we were tired of sandflies, fleas and mosquitoes and prancing up and down the sea coast after the Yankees, who always ran away before we could get near enough to get a shot at them.

At that time every company in the regiment had a wagon and a team of good mules and when we moved from one camp to another camp it required two or three trips with each company wagon to move the tents, cooking utensils and camp furniture. We were very rich in those days and never knew what it was like to be hungry.

We turned over our teams and wagon to the Quartermaster Department in Charleston and never saw them again.

On the morning of the 21st of July, we were marched to the railroad station and boarded a train waiting for us and were transported to Charleston. Leaving the train at St. Andrew's station, we marched through the city to the depot of the Northeastern railroad. There we were again placed on the cars and conveyed to Florence and thence to Wilmington, Weldon, Petersburg, and Richmond. We arrived at the latter place on the 24th day of July, 1862. Nothing worthy of note occurred on the route.

When the regiment received orders to prepare to deploy to Richmond, everything was topsy-turvy.

In camp some of the men tried to get leave to go home for a few days. Others wrote to home folks to meet them at the railroad stations where the train passed. All were doomed in disappointment, for instead of the Seventeenth regiment being routed via Columbia and Charlotte, it was detoured via Florence and Wilmington, etc. We thought it a mean trick, for we knew that the home folks would be at the several railroad stations with well filled baskets of good eats for us. However, the Hampton legion, which was sent by Columbia and Charlotte, were lucky, as they got the good things intended for us.

Installment III

On arriving at Richmond the regiment was marched about two miles and went into camp at the old fairgrounds, waiting until the remaining regiments, composing the brigade arrived from South Carolina.

I might as well state here before I forget it, that the brigade was composed of the 17th, 18th, 22nd and 23rd regiments, and the Holcombe legion; also one company of field artillery, the Macbeth Battery commanded by Captain Boyce. All these were from South Carolina and under the command of Brigadier General N. G. Evans.

While camped here a part of the regiment had its first skirmish on Virginia soil. The "casus heel" was as follows: There was a place near the camp where a man sold whisky. His way of dispensing it was through a window in his home. He would pour out the drinks and hand them through the window, always getting his pay first. His stock in trade consisted of a two gallon jug. Two men in the regiment, Dan Morgan and Green Poole, devised a plan to capture the jug. Going to his place, and calling for a drink, Poole gave the man a five dollar bill to get his payout of and as the old fellow went into an adjoining room to change the money, Poole followed him to get the change coming to him. In the meantime, Morgan got busy, climbed in the window, grabbed the jug and made for the camp.

When the old fellow returned to the window, he missed his jug and saw Morgan running off with it. He gave chase. It was "nip and tuck'." When Morgan got to the camp he ran into a tent and the old fellow misjudging the tent Morgan entered, rushed into a tent near it, and collared Elias Ramsey, who was coming out and struck him.

Ramsey knocked him down and got on him. Hill Young, standing near attempted to pull Ramsey off him. Some others, thinking Ramsey and Young were in a fight, joined in and before it was over, about twenty men were in the mix-up. When the smoke of battle cleared up about a dozen of the men stood there with bloody faces without knowing why they got into the affray. The bootlegger escaped at the commencement, unscathed. Morgan and Poole kept the jug without getting in the mix-up.

On the 28th day of July we broke camp and marched about eight miles below Richmond and went into camp between the Darbytown road and the James river. This camp was named "Camp Mary" in honor of Mary McMaster, wife of Lieut. Col. McMaster. While camped here we were engaged a good part of the time in throwing up breastworks in the direction of Malvern Hill. The regiment would march to where we had to work and remain until late in the afternoon and then return to camp. A detail left at the camp would cook and bring dinner to those at work.

On the 10th day of August the brigade was ordered to make a reconnaissance in front to Malvern Hill and feel for the enemy. We were deployed in the left of Darbytown road and struck the enemy's line about sundown near the edge of a piece of woods. After a few shots the enemy fell back and after dark we advanced through an open field in our front, about a hundred yards. Here we halted and waited for the 18th regiment to get into position on our right. While we were lying in line of battle, two regiments of Yankees in our front while getting in position, ran amuck of each other in the darkness and opened fire, each mistaking the other for Confederates. After, considerable firing, some one of them called out: "cease fire, you are killing your own men."

Up to this time we thought it was the 18th regiment engaged with the enemy. We fell back to the edge of the woods and remained under arms until morning, when we discovered that the enemy had evacuated their line and gone under cove of their gunboats. There wee no casualties in our regiment in this affair, but I saw some dead horses and two dead Yankees when we advanced through the open field.

We remained here all day and next morning went back to Camp Mary. In the evening, the regiment received orders to hold itself in readiness for marching orders at short notice.

On August 12th we got marching orders and early on the morning of the 13th we broke camp and took up the line of march to RIchmond, where we arrived about 8 o'clock. After remaining at the railroad depot a very short time we were placed on the cars-freight boxes- and transported to Gordonsville. We passed through a heavy rain and thunderstorm while in route. Arriving at Gordonsville in the afternoon, we camped that night near the depot and the next day were marched two or three miles west and camped near Mechanicsville, remaining in camp here two days.

On the second day three days rations of flour and fresh beef were issued to the men. As we had no cooking utensils we kneaded the flour into dough on pieces of the barrel head and cooked it by winding it around our ramrods and holding it over a fire. We broiled the beef on flat rocks with which ground was covered by heating them in the fire and placing the beef on them.

The brigade was assigned to General Longstreet's corps. We broke camp and took up the line of march on the 10th day of August on the Rapidan road. We left all extra baggage, such as knapsacks, clothing, etc., at Gordonsville. Each private's equipment was reduced to a blanket, oilcloth, oversack, and canteen, besides his musket and cartridge box. The first night we camped near a creek by the side of the road. The next morning we continued the march, arriving at the Rapidan river on the 18th and remaining there that night and the next day. Again taking up the line of march, we crossed the Rapidan river on the forenoon of the 20th of August by wading it at Raccoon's Ford just below Stringfellow's mill. We continued the march toward the Rappahannock river. Our rations were getting short, as we had not drawn any since we left Gordonsville. However, the wagon train caught up with us and had our wants supplied.

Nothing worthy of note occurred thus far on the march until the evening of the 22nd when a Yankee spy, impersonating a courier for Gen. Longstreet brought an order to General Evans directing him to move his command to another road. The spy had not gone far before Evans received an order through an officer of General Longstreet's staff to press forward rapidly and engage the enemy before they crossed the Rappahannock river.

The spy was caught and tried by a drumhead courtmartial, convicted and turned over to Capt. Culp of Company "A" with orders to hang him. About this time some cavalry rode up and asked the captain to let them have the job, which he gladly granted. The spy was a nice looking boy of 20 years old, said he was from Ohio. He requested to be shot rather than he hanged but his request was denied.

Had we not been halted and lost some time in the confusion, very likely we would have captured several prisoners and part of the enemy's wagon train. As it was, our advance guard captured several prisoners and had a pretty heavy skirmish with the enemy before they crossed the Rappahannock river.

We continued the march, passing through Stephensburg about dark. We camped that night near the railroad station. The next morning the 23rd, the enemy having thrown up entrenchments on the opposite side of the river, a terrific duel took place between our artillery and that of the enemy. The object of the enemy was to keep us from crossing until they could burn the railroad bridge, in which they succeeded. Our brigade supported our artillery. That night we drew three days rations which amounted to about what one man could eat in a day. We spent the night at the same place where we entered the previous night.

After having made arrangements to send all the sick and the wounded of the previous day back to the hospital, we broke camp the next day about 10 o'clock and continued the march, crossing Hazel river, a tributary of the Rappahannock; also several creeks. On account of the swollen condition of the streams, our progress was somewhat retarded as we had to wade them. Nevertheless, we reached Jeffersonton in the afternoon and went into camp for the night=not far beyond the town. The next day, the 25th, it rained all day, but we continued the march and could see at times the enemy's wagon train in the distance on the opposite side of the river.

We camped at night in a clearing and soon had good fires started from dry bush, preparatory to drying our wet clothing before going to sleep.
The enemy locating our position by the light of our camp fires commenced to shell us from the opposite side of the river. We were ordered to extinguish the fires and sleep that night on the ground in wet clothes.

Next day we crossed the Rappahannock at Hinson's Ford by wading and camped near Orleans.

Longstreet's corps of which we were a part, was now keeping in close touch with General T. J. Jackson. Passing through Orleans we camped the next night near White Plains, remaining there until 10 o'clock the next day-continuing the march we arrived at Thoroughfare Gap in the afternoon and camped in an apple orchard.

Early next morning, the 29th of August, we resumed the march, passed through the gap, which is a narrow defile about fifty yards wide and half a mile long. At the further end of this gap a part of the corps had had an engagement with the enemy on the previous day. Several of the enemy's dead were still lying there unburied. We could hear cannonading all day in our front or rather in the direction of Manassas Junction.

We were hurried on and reached the Warrentown turnpike at Gainesville-advanced by it to near Groveton, where we were placed on Jackson's right. We were deployed to the left, at right angles to the turnpike and supported General Hood's brigade during the evening of the 29th.

Saturday morning, August 30th, about 9 o'clock the regiment got rations while lying in the line of battle. The ration was roasting ears, of which each company got two water buckets full. We ate the roasting ears with a relish as most of them had eaten nothing since leaving Thoroughfare Gap the day before.

A large part of the day of the 30th was consumed in arranging the line of battle for the final struggle. The battle was opened about 3 o'clock in the afternoon by the Confederates advancing on General Pope's (U.S.) lines. The fighting was fierce and lasted until after sundown, when Pope's lines were completely shattered and driven off the field.

Evans' brigade was thrown against one of the strongest points in the Federal lines. It was a hill covered with field batteries supported by two heavy lines of infantry. They succeeded in breaking the Federal lines but it was at a fearful sacrifice.

Colonel Means was mortally wounded and died the next day. In some of the company of the Seventeenth Regiment not an officer was left unhurt. The regiment lost 34 killed on the field and 183 wounded-some of them mortally. About dark the regiment was relieved and those that came through safe began looking after their friends who were either killed or wounded. This was a sad part of it all.

Installment IV

On the next day the 31st of August (Sabbath) we remained on the battle-field all day.

A detail of two men from each company was made (of whom the writer was one) to bury the dead and collect together the wounded. We buried the dead in one grave-a trench about thirty feet wide, seven feet long and two feet deep. The bodies were placed side by side, according to the letters of the companies. We put some brush over their faces and filled in with earth. After this we brought up the wounded to the brigade field hospital, which was a tent, in a patch of woods.

The surgeon used the tent to operate in, and when they amputated a limb they threw it in a pile in the corner of the tent. I saw in the pile several legs with the shoes still on the feet.

After burying the dead I put in the balance of the day going over the battlefield. The field strewn with dead and wounded, many dead horses, broken cannon and small arms was sickening to look at, so much so I never cared to go over another. Sometimes I wish I had never gone over this one.

After the Confederate killed were buried and the wounded gathered up and cared for, on September 1st we began the march in the direction of Chantilly Courthouse. We passed through the battlefield where Jackson's corps had fought on the 29th and 30th of August. The enemy's dead were still lying on the field. In places the ground was strewn with dead men, and the weather being very hot decomposition was setting in and the stench at times was sickening.

We could hear cannonading all day in our front. We camped that night not far from Chantilly

Courthouse and remained there all the next day- the 2nd of September.

The enemy having got too close to the fortifications around Washington, to expect further success, General Lee decided to invade Maryland. All the sick were sent to the rear and the companies reorganized.

I should have stated that after the death of Col. Means, Lt. Col McMaster was promoted to colonel, R. S. Means to lieut. col and J. R. Culp Captain of Company "A" became major.

Everything being in readiness, we continued the march in the direction of Leesburg, after drawing three days of rations of beef and "hardtack."
The latter was crackers baked so hard that we had to soak them in water to eat them with any degree of satisfaction.

We arrived at Leesburg on the evening of the 4th and camped at a big spring, which looked more like a mill pond than a spring. On the morning of the 5th we had marched only a short a short distance when we came to the Potomac river. We took to the water, which was pretty cold and about three feet deep and possibly 50 yards wide. We got over or through all right. This being the first time we had put foot on the enemy's territory or beyond the boundary of the Confederacy, we gave the "rebel yell." We continued the march leisurely during the day and after wading several creeks, camped for the night in a piece of woods near a large creek.

We broke camp the next morning at 8 o'clock and passed through a rather broken country. There were some fine fields of corn and also good apple and peach orchards along the road; but we were not allowed to molest them. Strict orders had been issued before we crossed the Potomac that no private property must be molested and this order was strictly enforced.

We camped the night of the 6th near Frederick City. The next morning, the 7th we continued the march and arrived at Frederick City about 10 o'clock. We went into camp in an open field on the bank of the Monocacy river between junctions of the two railroads.

We had drawn no rations since the evening of the 2nd and having been prohibited from foraging from the country through which we had passed, we were pretty well starved out. Our wagon train soon caught up and we drew good rations of flour, beef and Irish potatoes.

The next day we moved our camp about half a mile to a piece of woods near a branch. Here we tore up the railroad track and destroyed the iron railroad bridge over the Monocacy river. We lay in camp all day of the 9th and on the morning of the 10th of September broke camp and returned the march on to Hagerstown pike road, passing through Frederick City.

All the stores were closed and the streets deserted.

One lady showed her loyalty to the Union by waving the stars and stripes from the second story of a dwelling as we were passing. Our color bearer waved the stars and bars at her in return and the men all cheered.

We passed through Middletown and camped for the night not far from South Mountain. Next morning the 11th we continued the march on the same road--crossed South Mountain, passed through Boonsboro and camped for the night near a toll gate on the pike. Next day we passed through Hagerstown and Funktown and went into camp about half a mile beyond the latter place on the banks of Antietam creek or river.

The country between Frederick City and Hagerstown was very hilly and at places the mountain scenery to the north was grand. The water was limestone and while cold, was not very palatable to men used to freestone water. There were some fine orchards on the side of the road.

We saw very few of the citizens. It looked as if most of the people had left their homes, taking with them their livestock and all domestic animals. All stores in the villages and towns were closed.

The road (or turnpike) over which we marched was fine. All streams had bridges and there were no mud holes, consequently the command "prepare for wading" was unheard.

We remained in camp at Funktown until the morning of the 14th of September (Sabbath). We drew three days rations on the evening of the 13th.

About 9 o'clock on the morning of the 14th we formed line and marched back over the same road we had travelled two days before. When we arrived at Boonsboro about 4 o'clock in the afternoon we could hear heavy firing in our front. We were hurried on to the pass in South Mountain and deployed to the left of the road near the crest of the mountain. We had barely time to form line when we were attacked by a part of General Reno's (U.S.) corps, the 127th Penn Regiment. They came at us in three separate times, all of which we drove back with heavy loss. We got so close when the second line made the attack that I could read the letters on their knapsacks, "127th Penn Regt." We held our position until after dark, repelling every charge on us.

We lost a good many men, killed and wounded. Some of the latter fell into the hands of the enemy. Lieutenant Colonel R. S. Means was wounded and taken prisoner. **This is where SBL was wounded.** S. Robert Lathan, author

During the night, the fighting having ceased, we were quietly withdrawn toward Boonesboro.

The next morning the regiment fell back in the direction of Sharpsburg arriving there in the afternoon. Here we placed in position on the south of Boonesboro road parallel to Antietam creek.

Only a little artillery firing was done on the 18th. The enemy seemed to be feeling their way. On the morning of the 18th the firing of the artillery became heavy and lasted all day. We were moved further down the road and supported General Hood's division. Both the infantry and artillery fighting was heavy during the 16th and 17th.

On the 18th neither side made any show of advancing. We lay all day on our arms and that night quietly with drew and crossed the Potomac, at or near Williamsport into Virginia.

Installment V

After crossing the Potomac river we remained all the next day in camp near the ford. On the following day we moved to near Martinsburg on the Occoquan river. Here we went into camp and remained about a week. Next, we were moved to a point near Winchester, VA preparatory, as we thought, for going into winter quarters.

The regiment had been on the march continuously since the morning of the 13th of August when we broke camp below Richmond, and the men were about fatigued out. Their clothing dirty and ragged. They had not even made a change of underwear. It all had been left at Gordonsville, Va. A at the beginning of the campaign.

After getting our baggage from Gordonsville and scrubbing up we felt and appeared like new men.

Most of the sick and broken down who had been left behind from time to time returned to the camp at Winchester.

The only thing that happened while here worthy of note was a review of the Army of Northern Virginia by General Lee. The review lasted nearly all day. I have no idea how many men were there but the number ran into the thousands.

There was nothing spectacular about the review except when these battle marred Confederates passed the reviewing stand and gave the "rebel yell" it was an inspiration.

We remained in camp at Winchester four to five weeks-drew good rations and nothing to do in the way of military duty except serve on details to cut fire wood.

On November 10th, the brigade (Evans) was ordered to Mississippi but the order was soon afterwards countermanded and the brigade was ordered to Eastern North Carolina.

In a day or two we broke camp at Winchester, Va. and took up the line of march down the Shenandoah valley towards Front Royal. During the day we waded a fork of the Shenandoah river and found the water cold. We camped the first night not far from where we waded the stream and close to Front Royal. Continuing the march next morning we crossed the Blue Ridge mountains at a gap-the name of which I have forgotten, and during the day we waded a tributary or rather one of the head streams of the Shenandoah. The water was very cold. After marching about twenty-five miles we camped for the night. Next morning we reached the railroad, not far from Culpepper Courthouse, and went into camp.

The country between Winchester and Culpepper Courthouse had been overrun several times by both armies and looked rather desolate in places. The marching was easy as the weather was cool and the road good.

After remaining in camp at the railroad part of two days, we marched to Culpepper Courthouse and halted and stacked arms in the middle of main street about sunset and remained there until near midnight.

The night was bitter cold and the regiment procured into use a big pile of wood that was near us and soon had big fires burning in the middle of the street.

About midnight we were placed aboard freight boxes and proceeded to Weldon, NC via Gordonsville, Richmond and Petersburg, VA.

Soon after leaving Culpepper Courthouse it commenced to snow nearly all day.

The men had no way of getting any fire in the box cars and the only way they could keep warm was to close doors tight to keep out the air as much as possible and all huddled up together somewhat after the manner of hogs.

On arriving at Weldon, the regiment remained a day or two and went to the Halifax Courthouse, where we remained but a short time before proceeding to Tarboro. We remained at Tarboro about a week, after which we went into camp near Weisses Fork, about four miles from Kinston, where we remained until December 1.

In the meantime General Foster (U.S.) was marching with a large force against Kinston, from the opposite side of the river (Neuse). We were in danger of being cut off and captured. The only thing left for us was to fall back on Kinston, which we did, across Falling Creek and camped for the night.

On the morning of the 13th we started out again and went on opposite Kinston and out on the New Front road where there was some skirmishing going on with the enemy.

About the time we got to the firing line our forces commenced falling back toward Kinston. We marched about a mile from Kinston and waited for reinforcements, which did not come up. After a few rounds had been fired from each side we fell still farther back near the river at a church and remained there all night.

Early on the morning of the 14th (Sabbath) the skirmish lines of both sides opened fire and a skirmish fight began. After a short while the enemy advanced in heavy column and forced out skirmishers back to the main line, which was formed at the church. In a few minutes the fighting began in earnest and lasted until about 12 o'clock. The enemy in the meantime having been reinforced, endeavored to get between us and the bridge over the river and cut us off. We fell back across the river and endeavored to destroy the bridge, but were only partially successful.

After crossing the river, we made a stand awaiting the enemy to make an attack on us. After waiting some time the enemy showing no signs of advancing, we took the road leading to Goldsboro and continued the march into the night.

Early in the morning of the 15th we formed a line of battle across the road and lay there all day. The enemy did not follow us but went in the opposite side of the river to Goldsboro.

After dark we marched on in the direction of Goldsboro, arriving at Mosely Hill on the morning of the 16th. We lay there all day and until after midnight when we were placed on the cars and landed at Goldsboro, about sunrise on the morning of the 17th. We drew rations and remained here about three hours. Then we were again placed on the cars and taken back to the railroad bridge over Neuse river.

The enemy had burned the railroad bridge and was formed in line of battle on the south side of the river. We were marched up the river to a bridge crossing where the balance of the brigade was already in line of battle and were formed on their right and ordered forward. When we got to the top of the hill behind an embankment of the railroad the enemy poured the shells into our lines heavily while we were getting into position.

It was now getting dark but we could see the enemy in heavy column on the move. We lay in our position all night. It was bitter cold and we had no way to warm ourselves. The Yankees seemed to have accomplished their purpose by burning the railroad bridge and quietly retired during the night.

The next morning we were drawn across the river and went into camp where we remained until the 23rd of December (1862). Then we boarded the cars and went to Goldsboro, then to Kinston and camped near Kinston and remained there until the 28th, when we were moved about four miles above Kinston on the Snow Hill road and went into camp.

We got some wall tents while there, the first tents we had since we left Richmond on August 12.

While we were camped here there was a heavy fall of snow. It was about a foot deep all over the ground.

Several of the men of different regiments of the brigade engaged in a regular snowball battle: the fight was conducted after the manner of a regular battle. The commanding officers were on horseback. Couriers were hurried to and fro and there was signaling by flags, etc. The casualties were few, but the fun great.

Also while we were camped at Kinston, Col. McMasters was placed under arrest by General Evans, and the regiment as an appreciation of the colonel bought a fine horse and presented it to him.

On the 5th of February we got orders to be ready to move and on the next day, broke camp and marched to Kinston, where about dark we boarded the cars for Goldsboro. We got to Goldsboro about sunrise the next morning. It was fearfully cold and as we had no way to have fires (we were always moved in boxcars) some of the men came near freezing. We left Goldsboro next morning and got to Wilmington that afternoon.

We remained in Wilmington that night and the next day, which was Sabbath. Some of the men attended church in the city, some looked for spiritual things in other places and others slept all day. Monday morning we took the march for Top Sail Sound about ten or twelve miles below Wilmington, on the Plank road. We arrived there in the afternoon and went into camp, which was known as Camp Jenkins.

We had a fine time while here, very little to do except light guard duty, and occasionally were engaged in throwing up the breastworks. We feasted on oysters while here, as there was an abundance of them to be had in the sound.

On the 3rd of March we moved from Camp Jenkins to Camp Benbow, on Murfreesboro Sound, about seven miles southeast of Wilmington.

This was a great place for fish. While camped here we had a general inspection near Wilmington. We marched there and went through inspection ceremonies and returned to camp that evening pretty well fagged out.

We remained at Camp Benbow until about the 17th of March, 1863, when we were again moved to about two miles east of Wilmington to Camp Whiting, we were ordered to East river and left early in the morning. It rained on us nearly all day. We got through in the afternoon and camped in the open for the night, which was pretty rough on us as we had our tents behind at Camp Whiting. It rained on us all the way back but we had our tents to shelter ourselves in when we got to camp.

Why we were sent to East river through the rain, kept there one night and marched back through the rain was one of the many such things that the privates never could understand.

We remained at Camp Whiting three weeks, when we broke camp on the 11th of April and marched back to Camp Jenkins, where we first went into camp after leaving Kinston. We got there in the afternoon.

While here there was a detail of men made every day to go to the Sound and catch fish for the use of the regiment. This was one detail the men were generally glad to get on. They used some seines and would catch enough in a few hours to feed the whole regiment. While camped around Wilmington part of the regiment did provost guard duty in the city.

A rather amusing incident happened when the regiment was returning to camp after the general inspection near Wilmington. Our camp was near a big creek and the road ran parallel to it for some distance. When the regiment got opposite to the camp several men fell out of ranks and crossed the creek on a footlog–expecting to fall in with their companies when the regiment came back after crossing the creek on a bridge about half a mile below. The colonel halted the regiment after crossing the bridge and had rolls of the company called, and the absentees noted. Thus the footlog party was caught–and put on extra duty. That night the old style regimental guard was relieved and these men put on guard duty as a punishment. About 10 o'clock at night, they commenced to call for "Corporal of the guard post No.–" in about a minute another called, "Corporal of the guard post No. so and so until all on post were calling. The colonel came out of the tent and ordered the captain of the guard to make the men keep quiet as he wanted to sleep, the guards took up the refrain "So do I" and between the call of the corporal of the guard and "So do I" the noise was so great the colonel had to give it up and relieve the guard from further guard duty that night.

Installment VI

On the morning of April 23rd, at dress parade, orders were read for the men to hold themselves in readiness to move on notice. On the evening of the 24th we drew two days rations, and early on the morning of the 25th broke camp and marched to Wilmington, arriving there about the middle of the day. We were soon placed aboard the cars and that evening about 4 o'clock left for Florence, SC where we arrived about daylight.

Florence at that time was a small village of about seventy-five or a hundred inhabitants. There were no streets, the houses were built along the public road and railroad. We immediately left Florence via the Northeastern railroad and late in the evening were disembarked about four miles from Charleston at Camp Beauregard. We remained there two or three days, when we broke camp and marched to and through Charleston, crossing the bridge over the Ashley rive and camping near the station on the Savannah and Charleston railroad. There we remained two days and then moved our camp further down the railroad to Camp Means.

The water was very bad ad good many of the men were taken down with dysentery. None of the cases proved fatal, however.

Blackberries were ripe and we could buy any amount of them from the Negroes at a small price.

We remained here until the evening of May 4, when we were moved to Secessionville on James Island.

After we had been here a few days the Yankees made a landing at Legaresville on Johns Island. The Seventeenth regiment, together with some other troops, was marched to Johns Island to attack the enemy.

We marched to St. Andrew's depot, placed on board and conveyed to Rantowles station, arriving there about sunrise the following morning. As soon as we got off the cars we formed into line and marched out on the Church Flats road. We crossed the Stono river on a drawbridge, which was built by some of the men of our regiment when we were first stationed on Johns Island.

Continuing the march, we passed by old Camp Pillow, where we had camped about a year before, and camped for the night a few miles from Haul Over bridge.

We learned that night that the Yankees had left the island and returned to their transports. Early the next morning we commenced the retrograde march after marching all day arrived at Secessionville about 9 o'clock in the evening and went into camp near one of the bomb proofs.

These bomb proofs were built somewhat like a storm pit. They were large enough to hold two thousand men or more, and were intended as a protection to the infantry when the enemy would shell their position from their gunboats and also from their heavy batteries on Johns Island.

We had to take to these bomb proofs once or twice while here and found it very disagreeable on account of the bad air when full of men and also for want of light.

On the 15th day of May the regiment got marching orders, and on the morning of the 18th we left Secessionville for Jackson, Mississippi.

We broke camp early in the morning and arrived at Fort Johnson, where we took a steamboat for Charleston, making the trip in a heavy wind and rain storm, arriving at East Bay about 10 o'clock. Marching through the city to the South Carolina railroad depot we boarded the train for Augusta, leaving about 12 o'clock. We arrived at Augusta about sundown the same day and left immediately over the Georgia railroad for Atlanta, reaching there the next morning, the 19th. We got to Montgomery in the afternoon, and went thence via Selma to Meridian, Mississippi, and from there to Jackson, going into camp at the Pearl river, about two miles from the city.

While passing through Georgia and Alabama the ladies would be out in goodly numbers at the stations when we would stop, and would frequently throw bouquets to the men with their (the ladies) names and addresses attached. One of these bouquets fell into the hands of Lieutenant Stephenson, who, on arriving at Jackson, wrote to the lady whose name was attached to it. They got up a regular correspondence. Later Stephenson got a furlough and visited at her home. An engagement followed and after the war was ended, they were married.

We remained in camp near Jackson a few days, when we were moved across the Pearl river, through and beyond the city, and went into camp in a piece of weeds near the insane asylum. Here we remained about a week, when we were moved nearer the Pearl river.

We had nothing to do while here and would pass most of the time bathing in the river or seeing the sights in the city.

There had been a battle fought here in May. The enemy had captured and occupied the town, burned several large warehouses filled with commissary stores and also destroyed the railroad bridge over the Pearl river.

We remained in this camp until the afternoon of June 22nd. On June 20th all extra baggage had been sent to the rear in charge of a non-commissioned officer and two privates, and on the 22nd the regiment moved out in light marching equipment on the road leading to Canton and went into camp at Christian Chapel church where it remained through the balance of the day.

While here we were paid two months salary.

The next morning about sunrise, we resumed the march on the same road and that afternoon went into camp near Livingston, where we remained about a week.

At Livingston the regiment was assigned to Major General French's division. In this division was an Arkansas regiment, the 9th, and a company belonging to this regiment was from Drew county. In it were a great many men who had formerly gone from Chester county. This coincidence gave pleasure to both parties as they could renew old friendships and talk over their war experiences.

We remained here until the 1st of July, when the march was again resumed in the direction of Vicksburg. After passing through Brownsville we arrived within a mile or so of the Big Black river and went in to camp at the Birdstone plantation on the evening of the 3rd, remaining here all next day. We were ordered to be ready to move by midnight of the 5th in fighting trim.

On the morning of the 6th the march was resumed, as was thought to cross the Big Black river and attack General Grant's army in the rear. When we had gone about two or three miles the column was halted. Here the news was spread that Vicksburg had surrendered.

We lay on our arms until about day-light of the morning of the 7th, when the retreat was begun back to Jackson. We passed by Edward depot through Clinton and arrived at Jackson about sundown. We could hear fighting in our rear nearly all day. We were marched a short distance below the city and went back into camp on the Pearl river with about half the men broken down and half behind.

On account of the scarcity of water, the dust made by the moving wagon train and artillery, the extreme heat (the thermometer must have been up in the 90's), this was one of the hardest marches we ever experienced.

All the broken down men from the day before got into camp the next day and the next morning about daylight the regiment was marched out to the breastworks around the city and placed in the trenches in line of battle. We remained there all that day and night awaiting the approach of the enemy.

About 8 o'clock on the morning of the 10th the Yankee pickets opened fire on our lines west of the city and kept up the firing all day both with artillery and infantry. This was kept up with more or less intensity until the night of the 16th. Then it became apparent that our army was being flanked and we were withdrawn across the Pearl river. We marched out on the road leading to Brandon, passed through there and about two miles beyond and camped for the night. The next morning we resumed our march on the Hillsboro road. During the day it rained, making the road muddy and the marching tiresome.

We went into camp near a creek in a piece of woods and remained here until the next morning. On the afternoon of the 21st, we started out again and after marching four or five miles on the road heading towards Meridian took the Morton and Raleigh road and camped near a stream called Baker's creek. There we remained all of the 21st and 22nd.

There had been a battle fought at Baker's creek sometime previous and there were still to be seen some of the fruits of it. We remained here until he 24th, when we marched out in the direction of Enterprise and camped at a big spring near Beaverdam creek. On the 4th of August the regiment broke camp and marched to Forest Station on the Southern Mississippi railroad where we arrived about the middle of the day. Here we drew three days rations and shortly after the men had finished cooking them a train rolled up and took all the officers horses, medical stores and camp equipment aboard and shortly after the men were placed aboard the cars and headed for Meridian.

This ended our Mississippi war experience. We arrived at Meridian during the night and remained until morning when we left for McDowell's landing on the Tombigbee river, reaching there about midday.

Not long after leaving Meridian Major Dye, a member of Company "D" was accidentally killed. He was sitting on a flat car with his feet hanging over the side, eating his breakfast. He was struck be a projecting rock in a cut, knocked off and run over by the cars. He lived about an hour.

Shortly after we get to McDowell's landing, we were placed on a boat and in about an hour landed at Demopolis, Ala. Here we entrained and arrived at Selma about dark.

The extra baggage that had been sent to the rear when we left Jackson for Vicksburg had been stored here and was now turned over to the men. We left Selma by steamboat for Montgomery, in the night. We reached there the next morning and remained all that day and night and left there for Opelika by rail.

From Opelika we went to Columbus, Ga., where we remained all night--the next day we left Columbus and arrived at Macon about the middle of the day and remained until late in the afternoon. Next we went to Savannah, arriving there next morning, August 9 (Sabbath). The day was spent in sleeping and resting up or strolling over the city.

Installment VII

Early the next morning we left Savannah for the Isle of Hope and after marching some distance over the shell road were halted and went into camp near the Skidaway river. While here clothing and shoes were issued to some of the men who were in bad need of them.

About the middle of the day of the 26th the regiment broke camp and marched to Savannah. It rained heavily part of the way and was raining when we got there in the afternoon. We lay around the depot of the Charleston and Savannah railroad until after dark when we boarded the cars and were landed at the St. Andrews depot in Charleston, the next morning. We lay at the depot until after 12 o'clock and then marched across the bridge over the Ashley river and through the city in a heavy rain to East Bay Wharf. Here we boarded a steamboat and were landed at the wharf at Mt. Pleasant. It was still raining hard when we were marched off the wharf to the edge of town where we camped for the night.

The next morning the 29th we marched up along Shem's Creek about two miles to Lucas's Mills and went into camp a short distance beyond the mill and remained there until the last of September.

The only duty performed there was occasionally to guard the bridge connecting Sullivan's Island with the mainland.

On September the 30th the regiment broke camp and were marched six miles up the Georgetown road to Camp Nelson near the Episcopal church and went into camp.

During the stay here the men were daily employed throwing up breastworks and cutting down the timber in front of the earth works. We remained here until about the 10th of October when we marched to Mt. Pleasant and boarded a steamboat next morning and in about two hours were landed at the pontoon bridge over Wappoo Cut. We lay here (Sabbath) until noon when we were marched down near Pringle's pond on James Island.

The next afternoon we were marched to Secessionville and went into camp to some houses where we remained until the last of November.

While here the men were paid two months wages, viz twenty-two dollars. Also the Rev R. W. Brice of Chester county visited the regiment and preached several times.

On the last of November the regiment was relieved after Secessionville and was marched to Hatch's wharf, where we got on a boat after dark and were soon landed at Mt. Pleasant. We marched across the bridge to Sullivan's Island and down to near the commissary, two or three miles beyond Fort Moultrie. Here we went into camp in some houses vacated that day by a North Carolina regiment. The night was cold and the men got the full benefit of the cold sea breeze when crossing the bay and marching up the island.

We had a very good time while stationed here. The only duty was light camp guard and occasionally doing picket duty along the beach. We could also get boxes from home, which added materially to both the quantity and quality of our rations.

The regiment remained here until the 12th of February, 1864, when it was ordered to James Island. We marched to Mt. Pleasant, got on a boat about sundown and headed for the pontoon bridge over Wappoo Cut, but on account of the boat getting aground at the entrance of the cut we did not arrive at the bridge until after midnight. After landing we marched a mile or two on the road leading to Fort Pemberton and remained there the balance of the night and until about sundown the next day. Then we were marched back to the pontoon bridge, placed on a boat, taken across the bay and landed at the wharf of the Savannah and Charleston railroad. Next morning we boarded the cars for Green Pond station on the South Carolina railroad, and got there about the middle of the day. After getting off the cars we marched a short distance and camped for the night.

The next morning we were formed into line and marched about two miles up the railroad and went into camp, where some cavalry had winter quarters, but had moved out a day or so before.

While located here the men were employed at all kinds of duty. Sometimes they were cutting out and building roads, at other times doing picket duty and again they were throwing up breastworks in the vicinity of Combahee river, and as far south as Pocataligo.

Frequently when we were near the Combahee river, wild ducks would come to the ditches in the rice fields, after dark, by the thousands. The noise they made while flying sounded like a moving train. They would move off again about day light. The Negroes living around there said these ducks were returning from farther south where they spent the winter and were going north. I don't know if this is true or not; but I do know that there was many a duck in the bunch.

After remaining here until the middle of April the regiment was ordered to North Carolina. We boarded the cars at Green Pond and about the middle of the day landed at Charleston and left Charleston the same evening, the 18th of April, via the North-Eastern railroad. We got to Florence the next morning and left in the afternoon for Wilmington, but after going as far as Mars Bluff, for some cause, returned to Florence, where we remained until near daylight. We started again and got to Wilmington about the middle of the afternoon of the 19th. It rained all day and the cars were leaky, which made it very disagreeable.

After getting off the cars the regiment marched two or three miles north of the town and camped for the night. The next morning we marched back to the depot, as it was thought to go to Weldon N.C; but the order was countermanded and the regiment marched back to Camp Burgwyn, the old winter quarters of a North Carolina regiment. After remaining there a few days the regiment was sent to Tarboro to act as a guard in transporting some prisoners, captured near Newbern, N. C. to Andersonville, Ga. After taking the prisoners to Charleston we turned them over to other troops and returned to Wilmington. Here we remained until about the middle of May when we were ordered to Petersburg, Virginia. The regiment left Wilmington about sundown and got to Weldon in the night. We left there the next day and got to Petersburg after dark. Then we marched out a short distance east of the town to where a part of the brigade was camped and remained there until morning.

On the evening of the 19th the regiment was moved near the Appomattox river and placed behind some breastworks, expecting to remain here all night. After dark orders came to prepare three days rations and about 10 o'clock at night we left camp and marched back to Petersburg. Crossing the Appomattox river, we took the turnpike and halted near General Beauregard's headquarters. Here we lay until near daylight, when we were ordered to the support of a battery, which was engaging the enemy near Howlet's farm.

When it got near where the enemy was stationed, we double-quicked, passed our line of breastworks and went through a piece of woods to a ravine and on up to the top of the hill. When we got in the open in full view of the enemy's pickets, we went on to our picket line, halted a few minutes, fixed bayonets and were ordered to charge at double-quick. When the regiment got to the enemy's picket line behind a fence they had all left except a few, and these were captured. The enemy made several attacks, endeavoring to retake the line, but were repulsed in every attempt with heavy loss. We remained in the trenches, occasionally moving our position either to the right or the left; but most of the time at the Howlet farm near the Howlet house we were engaged in picket firing and strengthening the breastwork. This continued until June 16th, when the whole brigade evacuated their lines and marched to Petersburg. We took the Jerusalem road, passed the cemetery, and halted near the breastwork. We remained here a short time and then were moved further to the right to the Tim Reaves house, and put in the trenches, after dark.

The next morning, the 17th of June, the men were put to throwing up a new line of breastworks, in the yard and garden of the Reaves house. In a few hours we were moved up about half a mile to an old line of breastworks near where the enemy had broken our line and were occupying that broken portion. During the night we were quietly withdrawn to an inner line of breastworks, which eventually became the permanent line of defense around Petersburg.

With the 18th of June, 1864, began the siege of Petersburg, which lasted until the 1st of April 1865, and during all this time, nearly ten months, it was a continued fight by day and night, with artillery and sharpshooters. The latter were paced at short intervals along the breastworks in which small port holes for their muskets to protrude through were made and it was generally death to the man that showed himself above the breastworks on either side, as both armies were similarly fixed. The sharpshooters would be relieved every two hours. The balance of the men would be in the trenches in sections during the day and night. Usually a regiment would be in the trenches about a week and be relieved when they would go to the rear and be held in reserve.

Installment VIII

After the 20th of June, 1864 there was a lull in the infantry firing around Petersburg. The artillery fire was constant on both sides until July 30th. The enemy sprung a mine under a portion of our line of breastworks on that day and the memorable "Battle of the Crater" followed.

The crater or mine, was a tunnel dug in our line and immediately under one of our forts, known as, the Elliot salient. This was east of the Jerusalem plank road and about three quarters of a mile southeast of Cemetery Hill. The main tunnel, after reaching the spots underneath where Pegram's battery of four guns was located extended about forty feet each way. The whole was in the shape of the letter "T".

It was said that there were five charges of 2,000 pounds of powder, each placed as follows: one at each end, one in the middle and one between each end and the middle point. About 5 o'clock a.m. the mine was sprung and Pegram's battery was blown up and every man killed or wounded.

Elliot's brigade was stationed as follows in reference to the fort, viz:

The 23rd regiment on the extreme right, the 22nd regiment next to the left of it and partly over the crater and to the left of it the 18th and to the left of the 18th was the 17th regiment and the 28th was on the brigade. The portion of the 18th and 22nd regiments that were contiguous to fort were almost annihilated.

In a few moments after the explosion the enemy opened up a terrific cannonading of our lines and at the same time made a vigorous assault of our line. They succeeded in getting into the breach made by the blow-up and thus captured a portion of the double line of breastworks adjoining the crater.

The endeavoring to recapture the works, a portion of the 17th regiment was cut-off and captured.

Soon reinforcements arrived and the enemy was driven back into the crater with immense loss in killed, wounded, and prisoners.

In many places it was a hand to hand fight. Our line having been completely restored before the night of the same day of the blow-up, each army was in the same position as before.

The next day the enemy sent a flag of truce, requesting permission to bury their dead, which was granted. They buried about 300 in the crater and 800 near it. The weather was hot, the graves were shallow and the stench from these bodies was most unbearable for some time.

We remained in the trenches performing the same duties as before until 13th of March, 1865, when the regiment was relieved and the whole brigade was marched some distance west of Petersburg to Burge's Mill, on Hatcher run. We remained here until about sundown of the 24th, when we marched back to Petersburg and the whole of the division (Bushrod Johnson's) at daylight of the 25th of March, in connection with General Gordon's corps, attacked the enemy's line at Fort Steadman near the Appomattox.

The fort was captured together with a good part of their line of defense adjoining and was held until about 11 o'clock, when the enemy massed a heavy force at this point and flanked our forces on both the right and left, thus compelling us to fall back. Col. McMaster was captured here.

The whole brigade went back to Burge's Mill, reaching there about day light of the 27th and the next day marched out on the Boydien road to a place called Sawdust Pie. Here the division was attacked by Sheridan's advance forces and a stubborn fight ensued.

Early the next morning we moved along the White Oak road parallel to the enemy and skirmished with him all day.

During the 29th it rained all day and on the night of the 30th of March we went into camp at Five Forks. The enemy having gone in the direction of the Dinwiddie court house, the next day our forces followed and camped in a piece of woods right near that place. We learned afterward we were partly within the enemy's line and practically surrounded by the enemy. We could not have any fires that night and before day next morning commenced a retreat towards Five Forks. We were pursued by the enemy and got to our camp of the night before at about 12 o'clock on April 1st.

The men were tired from marching and loss of sleep and very hungry and began to prepare their dinner; but had scarcely time to eat it before they were called out and formed in line of battle along the main Five Forks road.

Soon after getting in line the enemy rushed on our line in full force and the fighting was at close range and fierce. Our men held their ground and stubbornly held the enemy in check until about the middle of the afternoon, when Sheridan's whole forces came up. The fighting continued until we were completely overlapped by superior numbers, when we commenced to retreat by the right flank. We were in great danger of capture as we had stood our ground until it was almost too late to escape.

The rout of Pickett's whole command became general. Lieut Jno. R. Culp was wounded and taken prisoner. The command of the regiment devolved on Capt. E. A. Crawford, the ranking officer present.

After marching all night, the remnant of the regiment with the balance of the brigade reported to General Johnston near Ford's depot, and were marched across a creek and camped.

On the morning of the 3rd of April the retreat was continued in that direction of Amelia court house, taking the Namozine road at Namozine church in order to cross Deep creek at Brown's bridge. The brigade had a skirmish with the enemy's cavalry before getting to the bridge; the cavalry being easily dispersed.

The regiment moved hurriedly on to near Bull's bridge over the Appomattox. Next day we moved in the same direction and halted about four miles from Amelia court house where the road from Tabernacle church crosses the road to the court house. The enemy's cavalry made an attack on our forces by the way of the Tabernacle road, but were easily repulsed.

On the 5th the command marched through Amelia court house and continued until the afternoon of the 6th when it was placed in line of battle and drove back some cavalry skirmishers some distance. The brigade was then moved further on in the previous line of march and ordered hold in position on the edge of a piece of woods.

Late in the afternoon it moved forward in the line of battle with the whole division. As soon as the brigade got out of the woods in the open field the enemy's artillery opened on it and the brigade rushed across the field to a lane where a lot of wagons were on fire. Here the enemy made a vigorous attack on the left flank, completely routing the brigade. The men, after falling back a short distance, reassembled and joined the main column and arrived at High Bridge about midnight.

On the 7th we moved to Farmville and formed on the north side of the Appomattox. In the afternoon with the balance of the army, we left there, going in the direction of Lynchburg, continuing the march into the night. We moved out next morning, the 8th, and arrived near Appomattox in the afternoon and formed in line to meet a threatened attack of the enemy. Later we were moved to Appomattox Court House and again formed in line, the men sleeping on their arms. The next day, the 9th, with the balance of Lee's army we surrendered to General Grant. After the formality of paroling the men was over, we drew rations of crackers and meat from the Federals, and struck out in groups for our homes. Thus ended the war movement of the Seventeenth regiment South Carolina Volunteers.

In closing this sketch I want to say that in the spring of 1907 I wrote and published in the Chester Lantern a series of articles concerning the movements of the regiment. The present sketch is a revision of the former, eliminating some things and adding others.

In getting up the former sketch my memory was refreshed by J. T. Marion and S. Kitchen, who kept diaries; also by Capt. W. H. Edwards, W. O. McKeown, H. White and possibly others. These comrades are now dead and I mention this fact in appreciation of their memory.

There are a few of the members of the regiment now living and those alive are the very old men of the country.

The End.

1923

Mr. S. B. Lathan Talks Interestingly Of the Old Heyman Building, Etc.

By H. J. Hindman.

Spending a morning in the company with Mr. S. B. Lathan, of Chester, is better than keeping company with the best history books that deal with this section of South Carolina. There's the human interest side of his stories that are sadly lacking in the best histories written by the highest salaried writers in the country. We know because we've just finished about ten years of history reading, compulsory and otherwise, but one morning in the presence of that venerable and kingly old gentleman, Mr. Lathan, is like eating the dessert of a dinner.

We found all this out when we went to seek some information concerning one of the old landmarks of Chester that is soon to give way to the twentieth century mode of improvement. The old Heyman building standing on the corner of Walnut and Lancaster streets now occupied by the Carroll-Foote Grocery Co., after facing the storms of nigh on to eight-five or eighty-six winters and summers, will soon be replaced by a modern structure of brick and mortar.

"Well, now, that old place was built by the grandfather of Mr. William Nicholson, Sr., who for a number of years ran what is now the Myers Hotel. The old man," said Mr. Lathan, "built the place a good many years before the War between the States and it was standing there when the first railroad spike was driven in Chester, which was back in '51. After the South Carolina and Charlotte Railway (now the Southern) wound its way through the hills of Chester county. Mr. William Nicholson's grandfather built what is now the Myers Hotel and the business entered to the transient patronage. While in possession of the old building now occupied by Carroll-Foote, the proprietors operated a small boarding house upstairs and a grocery store down stairs.

"At that time practically all of East Chester was wooded and only a few dwelling houses and probably one or two business houses stood where now is one of the most densely settled portion of the city.

"Then after the old man Nicholson built the Nicholson Hotel (now Myers), the old stand was sold to the father of Messrs. Sayling and Mose Heyman, and to Mr. Issacs Heyman, the uncle of Sayling and Mose. The place was run by these men from 1861 to 1872 or 1873, still remaining as a boarding house, except for the period of the war when both hotels were closed.

"At that time the population of Chester was in the neighborhood of 900 people, and most of the grocery houses of the city were located in that section of the city which is now east of the Southern railroad and occupying lots on Lancaster street. Where the Crosby Ware House now stands, were brick houses that were used as hospitals during the war. The main roads leading into Chester at that time were the Lancaster Road, the Columbia Road and the Saluda Road. The latter highway having obtained its name from the course it took at that time, coming into Chester from the Saluda country on the south and running on north of Chester.

"After the war, the building again resumed its business of housing boarders, using the upstairs for that purpose and the lower floor taking care of a dry goods establishment and a bar-room. Until recent years the old landmark that has for so many years called Chester its home was a part of the Heyman estate and until a few years before the death of Mr. Mose Heyman, was occupied by that gentleman and his family.

When asked if there were many houses in Chester that were older than the one under discussion, Mr. Lathan answered, "one or two" and named the Davega house on Pinckney street (now owned by Dr. W. B. Cox), and the old Hemphill place on West End.

Mr. Lathan likes to think of the amusing instances that he remembers of those days 'way back yonder. Recalling the difference in the means of transporting produce of those days and this, he related this one to us, chuckling. "Old Abe Smith who did hauling and draying in this part of the country back when the Seminole Indians of Florida got sorter restless in 1834, took a load of cotton to Philadelphia and while up there the Seminole War happened along and the government pressed Abe and his horses and wagon into service and sent him to Florida with a wagon load of army supplies. On the way down there, one of the horses became lame and Abe lost his horse. He put in a claim for it and was just about to get paid for the animal when the Civil War interfered and Abe never got a cent.

When the Railroad first put in its appearance around this part of the country, people used to camp alongside the tracks to get their first glimpse of the steel monster. Down at Blackstock, Mr. Lathan said, an old lady with her little boy came for some distance to see the passenger train on its first run. The train stopped and all the people including the old lady and her little boy were inspecting this novelty that breathed smoke and ate wood. When the engineer jumped into his cab and called for his fireman to get aboard, he gave two sharp jerks of the whistle cord, and, the shrieks reaching the little boy's ears set him wild and he started off for the neighboring hills with his mother in pursuit, calling "come back Johnny, come back Johnny." Mr. Lathan says he expects the boy is still running. At least he was the last time he saw him. This was back in the '50's.

When I asked Mr. Lathan how old he was he replied that he felt about forty, but that he was really 82 years of age. He says that those recollections are as if the happenings really occurred yesterday. He reminiscently stated that it seemed only a short time ago when he, after returning to his father's farm from a visit to Blackstock, his father had haulted him where he was cutting down a tree in the yard of his home and questioned him, "What news, son?"

"South Carolina passed the act of secession yesterday in Charleston," was the answer forth coming.

"Well," replied the father Lathan learning on the axe handles, "that means the end of slavery and beginning war and you and Will can get ready for it." That was sixty-five years ago and yet the gentleman with the kind old face could recollect the conversation.

He states that secession was very unpopular in this section of the state. *The Chester Standard* was the newspaper of Chester then and it was edited by Jack McDaniel. For awhile there were a series of letters appearing in the newspaper apparently from two individuals, one in favor of secession and one against it. The letter reached the point where people thought that the next communication would call for a duel (for those were duelling days then) between the two men. It seemed that the one standing against secession would always get the better of the other antagonist. When the veil was lifted, the two individuals were really one in the person of Dr. A. P. Wylie, father of Dr. Gil Wylie, and the author of the letters was himself, against secession and intentionally allowing the make-believe-author to get the worst of the argument.

I wish to thank Mr. Lathan for the information he gave me and for the most interesting interview that the visit afforded me. If these are any errors in this article I take the responsibility for them, since Mr. Lathan is usually accurate in the details of history, especially of Chester county history.

August 14, 1924.

W. W. Dixon Has A Talk With Mr. S. B. Lathan The Chester Reporter January 27, 1936

(W. W. Dixon In *Winnsboro News Herald*)

It is a privilege to visit Chester once a week and converse with the oldest and most outstanding citizen of Chester and Fairfield counties. By reason of strength, has reached the Biblical allotment of life and exceeded it by a quarter of a century of years, yet the erectness of his form, the texture of his skin, the timbre of his voice would not apprise a strong-hold of the great longevity of this revered friend, Samuel Boston Lathan, who on the second day of May will have reached his 94th birthday.

The first time we saw him was years ago at a public gathering at Blackstock, SC, in the woods near that town. Then he was in the meridian of his days. Not long ago we saw him occupying a seat of honor on the rostrum in the high school building in Chester, on the celebration of the 400th anniversary of the Miles Coverdale's translation of the Bible. Certainly of the honored ones upon that stage, no one presented a better appearance than he did. There was something about him distinctive upon the others-something Greek and philosophic, like Plato; or Conan and heroic like one of the Saranesca princes of Rome, as F. Marion Crawford can so delineate.

We conversed over an hour with the writer, last week, about many, many things, events, early customs, Indians, religion, politics, inventions, and the changes that have brought about in his time.

The town of Blackstock was named for Edward Blackstock, who became its first postmaster, October 1, 1804. Some times the office has been in Fairfield, and at other intervals, in Chester, as the boundary of the counties runs through E. M. Kennedy's store. He told of the building of the railroad; the time trains did not run on the Sabbath day. He was a Confederate soldier in Gov. John H. Means' regiment. Capt Beaty-long a merchant in Winnsboro, was his captain; he was wounded at South Mountain (Antietam). Was captured and carried a prisoner of war to Baltimore. Went to school as a boy to William Doaglass in 1849. His brother Robert Lathan, is a writer of history and government.

He spoke interestingly of courts and celebrated criminal cases with solicitors such as W. H. Brawley, C. D. Melton, Chalmers Gaston, Tom Dawkins, Mackey (not the judge), J. E. McDonald, Hough, Henry, J, Lyles Glenn, and Gist Finley.

And of political campaigns for Congress with such forensic orators on the hustings as W. W. Boyce, W. H. Perry D. R. Duncan, W. A. Barber, John J. Hemphill, T. J. Strait, Stanyarne Wilson, G. W. Shell, Joe Johnson, D. E. Finley, Stevenson and J. P. Richards.

Address and Reminiscences Samuel B. Lathan, Litt. D.

Delivered at Sesqui-centennial Celebration Hopewell A.R.P. Church July 27, 1937

...This talk was made without notes by Dr. Lathan at the age of 95!...

When the Roman gladiator came into the arena he turned to his audience and uttered these words, "O, Caesar, we who are about to die, salute you!" Today in meeting this group I shall somewhat paraphrase that sentence and say, "O friends of my former days, one who is soon to pass beyond the river, greets you!"

The other day when Mr. Kennedy came down to see me and told me he was expecting me here today and wanted me to make an address or speech, or to say something, I told him that I hoped to be here, but I would not make any speech; that I might say something, but whether it would be interesting or not, I did not know. I thought it might be with you somewhat as it was with Cato, a Black boy I heard once. A preacher in a different county from this had hired this boy Cato, and part of his duties was to drive the carriage for the family to go to church on the Sabbath day. One day, upon the Sabbath, as he was preaching he saw the boy had a piece of paper in his hand with a pencil figuring or writing something on that paper. After he went home the preacher called Cato and said, "I saw you with a piece of paper figuring or writing. What were you doing?" Cato said, "Boss, I was taking notes of your sermon." Cato pulled the paper out of his pocket and showed it to his boss. The preacher looked at the paper and found nothing on there except scribbling, hieroglyphics, or some kind of scratching. He said, "Cato, that is nothing!" But Cato said, "Boss, I thought that when you were saying it, them was your sayings!" So that is the way it may be with me.

I will say this, that I have nothing whatever prepared to say, because I could not write it off, and I could not see to read it if I had written it. But when I got out of the car down here, I looked around and saw the crowd of people standing all around, and the thought occurred to me, "What are these people doing here?" What are they coming here for?" Then I thought, "They have come here to celebrate, as a memorial, the one hundred and fiftieth anniversary of the building of a church here." Now, I look back over those one hundred and fifty years and think of the changes since those early days. What was around here at that time? There were no railroads in the world at that time. Two hundred years ago all of this country was occupied by Indians and wild beasts. And when you come to think of agriculture, they had only the most primitive things with which to cultivate the lands. There were no cultivators; there was not a thrashing machine, not a ginning outfit; no farm machinery as we have today. At that time there was not a telegraph office, no steamships. But away back in that time those old Scotch people who came here away from persecution, for liberty, for freedom of religion, for freedom of society, first thought not of material use, but they wanted a place where they could worship God. And I might ask you this question, why did they locate here? Well, there was no better place; there was none then and there is none now. It was known then as the Rocky Creek Settlement. About two hundred years ago some Scotchmen came down from the north, Pennsylvania and New York, and established a trading place down here near the mouth of Fishing Creek and Wateree Creek. Then, as well as now, money always attracted people, and these Scotchmen wanted to bring in others from the outside; they wanted business, trading. Others came down; and here they formed what is known as a settlement, and they called it a "society". With a Scotchman there were always certain things he wanted. The first thing was to educate his children. So they established communities for that. Another thing, he could spend the Sabbath as he liked; he could keep it as he liked to do. Another thing was that he could come into this settlement and with his neighbors and friends worship God. It was not long before they wanted a house down here where they could worship God. They met in an old place about three miles from the Catholic Church. They called it a "Meeting-house". That was always a Scotch name for it, - a meeting- house – to meet with God, and they wanted a meeting -house where they could worship God according to their own consciences. They built a church over there in that settlement and they called that church "Catholic". That word means "universal". It has nothing to do with the Roman Catholic Church. These people were Presbyterians of one kind or another. A few were Episcopalians and perhaps a few other denominations; but they all joined in with the Presbyterians. So they built that church and they agreed to worship there. In order to be in that church a man had to be orthodox, and he had to conform to that doctrine and to a Presbyterian Assembly. After they got the church they did not have it more than two years until the British came along and burned the church and put the preacher in jail.

Then these Scotch people fell back to the Society worship. The Society met on the Sabbath day. The Society came along about 1787, or something like that. They would have preaching in those communities or Societies, as they called them. They would meet together at some member's house and read a sermon and sing the Psalms. Sometimes they would end up in an argument, as Scotchmen could do. But they were always well posted in the Assembly doctrines.

Of those different denominations in this country there were Associate Reformed Presbyterian and there were Covenanters, and the Associate Presbyterians. Then the preachers from Scotland came, and all the people worshipped together. After the Revolutionary War each one of these denominations or groups wanted a preacher. They had several Societies, one over on Rocky Creek, another one in Fairfield County. They were to get a preacher, and they met at some place around here. After consulting together they decided to build some kind of house of worship here. So they built, and they called the place "Hopewell". The house was built here because it was more central for a large number of Associate Reformers. Besides those Associate Reformers, others came into it, and many perhaps did not come in with us.

After building the church down here at the right-hand corner of the grave-yard, they wanted to get a preacher. That meeting house was a log house, built of hewn logs, and in order to get it done they went at it in the proper way. They decided to build the church themselves, and they did build it, that log house down there.

Unfortunately preachers were scarce then, and they did not get a preacher for a year or two. But they get one finally, a man by the name of Boyce. He came here, but did not live long; he died of consumption. He boarded at Mr. David McQuiston's. I can not call his name now.

After Mr. Boyce died they got a young man from Pennsylvania by the name of John Hemphill. John Hemphill came here to this country just after the War, and he had a trade that he learned in Philadelphia; he was a tailor. But he always had in mind that he wanted to preach the Gospel, and he did preach the Gospel. After he was called they brought him down here to this church. Two men went after him, and he and his young wife road horse-back down here. It took several weeks, but we can now ride that distance in an automobile in a few hours or a day or two.

This young preacher and his wife settled down here and bought a place, which I believe is still in the Hemphill family. He did not live in this house, which is there now on this place, but lived in a house across the road. It was fashioned after no particular style, built of hewn logs. Mr. Hemphill's son said there would be no harm in worshipping in it, as there was nothing like it under the heaven or upon earth.

Mr. Hemphill's first wife was Jane Linn. His second wife was the widow Hemphill, no relation whatever. She was from down here in this country. Her first husband was a doctor. They raised a family, and he preached here, commencing in 1805, and kept on until 1833. After he died, which was probably about a year later, they got another preacher, Warren Flenniken, from North Carolina. He was a very eloquent man and a very great student. He was said to have been one of the signers of the Declaration of Independence of Mecklenburg County.

After Mr. Flenniken came the Rev. R. W. Brice, who came to Hopewell about 1850 and served until his death about 1878. Then is where my memory commences, with the third preacher. He did not preach at Hopewell until along in 1850. There was an interregnum between the end of

Mr. Flenniken's ministry and the coming of Mr. Brice. We had supply preachers that came in here and preached for us. The first preacher that I can remember is Mr. Brice. I must have heard Mr. Flenniken but I have no recollection of him whatever. But I do remember Mr. Brice. When he came in Hopewell this church building was not here. There was a brick church down there just northeast of the graveyard, and that is where Mr. Brice was installed and where he preached for awhile.

There were changes taking place. Nearly all of those men that had met here in those early days were dead. Their families, though, many of them, were still living here. And they had certain peculiarities, those people back there. When they built that church (I do not remember the first wooden church) - that old brick church - it had to be in a hot place, because they had no way to heat the building. I can remember when we went there to church and almost froze to death.

The Rev. Mr. Kitchens was a Covenanter. He always read his long sermons. I could always tell when Brother Kitchens was halfway through. He would use this phrase, "Friends, now just one more remark, for the sake of illustration, and I will be through." He would be half way through by that time.

The service opened in the morning with the reading of a Psalm and the explanation of it. Then they would sing a Psalm. The old pulpit was a great, high thing, with a sounding-board over the head. Then the singers sat below the pulpit. There were two who would lead the music, the presenter would read two lines and they would sing two. It would do you good to see those old men and women in those days singing those Psalms; they would throw back their heads and sing, and it was really worshipping God in singing.

Mr. R. W. Brice was a man who was very systematic in his ways. He had his regular times for visiting around in the congregation, calling out from the pulpit where he would visit on Monday, Tuesday and so on. Every other year he went the rounds and visited every family. Then he visited in sections, usually where they had those Societies, white and Black. If there were Black people in the congregation he expected them to come around and be taught passages of Scripture and the Shorter Catechism along with the whites. After he got through teaching he would go; he did not linger around. He came there especially for that work, teaching the Scriptures and the Catechisms. I can remember yet as a boy some of the questions he asked me from the Shorter Catechism, asking questions on that. Some of them were very remarkable. I can remember his asking a Black man who tempted Adam and Eve to sin? The man answered, "The Old Boy!"

In addition to that, Mr. Brice kept a record of every visit paid during sickness or at any other time. He kept a record of every child baptized and who the parents were. He kept a record of every marriage, who they were and where they were from. He kept a perfect record of everything for the whole time he was here, for over thirty years.

Some of these things seem strange to us in this day. Up until after the Confederate War I never heard a funeral preached in this church. These old Scotch Irish, if a corpse had been brought in here, would have got up and walked out, thinking it was too much like the Roman Catholics and preaching the departed out of purgatory. The body was brought from home, and rarely was there any service at the grave. After the burial was over the crowd would drift away. There were no flowers put on the grave.

Another thing. In the administration of the sacrament, they had long tables in front of the pulpit. The people in the congregation would rise and come up to the tables. The preacher would preach a long sermon; he would tell who ought to come to the table and who ought not to come, and go over all those things. They called it "fencing the table."

I do not know when the Negroes commenced joining this church, but I know when Mr. Brice was here there were Negroes in the church. I know that at one time we had as many as thirty or forty or fifty. When the sacrament was to be administered, the Negroes would come up last and take their seats at the communion tables. I remember seeing in those days, the Negroes walk up there. I remember their singing those Psalms with as much zeal and delight as the white people. I remember distinctly two people, old Tom Reid and his wife. I think he was a free Negro, but I do not know whether his wife was free or not. They both belonged to the church. I remember another Negro, Burrel Hemphill. These two men would come in leading the group, and to hear those people sing it was real music; they would carry all the parts. There was one Negro who had an especially fine bass voice. They would come in for family worship in the "boss" house. They kept up family worship as it was kept up by the white people, and when living with their bosses they would come in at night and in the morning also and join in with the family prayers. Then when they lived by themselves they would have family worship in their own homes.

I see a marker out there at the front of the church erected to the memory of Burrel Hemphill, a faithful slave. He was here when Sherman's army came through here. This army camped around this church or near this church. Burrel Hemphill belonged to Mr. James Hemphill, who was vice president of the bank here in Chester. The bank had gold and silver, and the soldiers of Sherman's army got the idea that Burrel had that money hidden, or knew where it was hidden. They tried to make him tell, and he would not tell if he knew, even though they threatened to take his life.

There are some other things I might tell you. People always came to church, rain or sun; the weather did not keep them away. At that time there was a mill down on the creek. There was a bridge across that creek, and if it rained it got that creek up and over the bridge. When the Creek was up we had to go around six or seven miles to get home. The distance was short, but they could not cross the bridge after heavy rains. But they came, back in those days, rain or shine, because they had to keep the Sabbath Day. But besides that, another way we kept the Sabbath was to study the Shorter Catechism, asking the questions around.

Another thing that happened. When they had these Society meetings they always announced the Sabbath before whose house they would meet next. One man in the neighborhood forgot to keep up with his Almanac and got the wrong day. The Society was to meet at his house that day, and when the crowd began to come the good lady of the house had scoured the house out to get ready for them for the next day. The man of the house had gone out to the neighbor's house to get a jug of whiskey.

They were very strict about violating the Sabbath Day, or with those who violated the Sabbath. They had a man up once for shooting a hawk on the Sabbath; they had him up before the Session of the church. He claimed it was a necessity, that the hawk was killing his chickens. But the man who was prosecuting him said that he was annoying the neighbors. The man said, "Well, brother, if you got close enough to that hawk with a stick, what would you have done?" The brother said he would have hit the hawk if he was killing his chickens. "Well" he said, "what was the difference? One would make a little more fuss than the other."

How Dr. Saml. B. Lathan, Chester U. C. Veteran, Spent Christmas 76 Years Ago

While musing the other day over the past, my mind reverted to a Christmas spent seventy-six years ago in Baltimore, Maryland. This was one of the most pleasant and unique of all the Christmas seasons I have enjoyed in my many years. You will very likely want to know what I was doing in Baltimore in 1862. Was I not in the Confederate army? Yes, but it came about in this way, on the first day's fighting (Sept. 14-'62) of the battle of Sharpsburg, Md., I was wounded severely and left on the battlefield, where I remained a week, then was taken a prisoner to Fredricktown, Md., with several other wounded prisoners, and placed in a temporary hospital where I remained three or four days. After that time was moved to a special hospital run by some ladies of the town of Fredricktown, but supervised by Federal officers. I remained here two weeks, when two ladies from Baltimore, Misses Cook and Brandon who were visiting the hospital, offered to take me to Baltimore and place me in a private home which offer I quickly accepted. After some parleying with the physician and warden of the hospital they finally got me out and moved me in an ambulance to the depot of the B. and O. railroad where we boarded the train and landed at our destination at about 8:00 P. M., and thence to the residence of Chas. Pepar, 814 West Baltimore street, where I remained until January 10, 1863.

Mr. and Mrs. Pepar had no children of their own. A niece of Mrs. Pepar lived with them, and through her kindness I became acquainted with many of the young people of that section of the city. I had been there only a day or two when a haberdasher came around and took my measure and fitted me out with a complete wardrobe of which I was badly in need. I had a great many visitors during my two and one-half months stay in the city and much kindness was extended to me. But to proceed with the Christmas of 1862. On the evening of December 24, I was invited to a six o'clock dinner at the home of Mr. Wm. Winston, a brother of Mrs. Pepar. The guests included only the immediate members of the connection besides myself. The dinner was sumptuous and delicious and was thoroughly enjoyed. Mr. and Mrs. Winston were most cordial and exerted themselves to make me feel at home. After dinner Mrs. Pepar, Julius Winston and myself went around to some of the stores to see the Christmas decorations which were varied and beautiful, all were illuminated with gas as electric lights were unknown. The one which was most admired was call "The White Store," everything in it was white, the sales ladies, flower girls and cash boys were all dressed in white as also the fixtures of the store. After returning to Mr. Pepar's home and retiring for the night my thoughts went to my home folks in South Carolina wondering if all was happiness there. I finally dropped off to sleep. After a good night's rest I waked up Christmas morning feeling fine. After dressing and looking around I found my room full of children's toys – viz., tin horns, false faces, dolls, etc., but it was not long before my bewilderment passed when some girls came in laughing at the joke they had played on me and took the toys to an orphanage nearby for its inmates.

After breakfast I took a ride over the city with some girls and boys, seeing the sights. We stopped at a photographer's and had a group picture taken. While in the studio I was introduced to an elderly lady. I talked with her for several minutes. She was interested in my wound and war experiences. When she bade me good-bye she put something into my hand. I dropped it in my pocket and when I got back into the carriage I found it to be a five dollar gold piece. After returning to my room and dressing I attended Christmas dinner at the home of Mrs. Carrington. It was an elaborate affair. It was served in courses, and it was nearly three hours before the dinner was ended. A large Confederate flag hung over the table as Mrs. Carrington and her guests were known as Southern sympathizers. A week afterward, on New Year's Day, January, '63, I was invited to another dinner party at the home of Mr. and Mrs. Chas. Bayne, a banker and broker. There I received the same gracious hospitality and elaborate entertainment. This ended my Christmas festivities.

A few days later I went to General Wool's office, who was commander of the district, to make my report which he required me to do every ten days of my presence in the city. He informed me he had been transferred to another district and Gen. Sickles had been assigned his place. As Gen. Sickles had lost a leg lately he would not be likely to allow me the freedoms of the city since he felt none too kindly about the Confederate side. He advised me to go across the lines as he was sending a boat across to City Point in a few days. I took his advice and the next day was driven in a carriage by Misses Cook and Brandon to Fort McHenry where Gen. Schenk gave me my parole across the lines. I bade my lady friends good-bye, then watched the carriage until it passed out of the gates to the fort and waved a last farewell.

Saml. B. Lathan.
December 22, 1937

The Chester Reporter, October 13, 1938

By Catherine Irwin

We sit and wish we could go to foreign lands to visit historical sights, but if we look around us we find them almost at our doorsteps. I wonder how many of us have been wandering around the Wylie Park and seeing the one grave there, casually wondered who it might be. Possibly it was just a passing thought until Mrs. Mary Ferguson and her helpers, in beautifying the park: made us more conscious that some loved one was buried there. My curiosity was way too assertive, so I called on Mr. S. B. Lathan, and he so kindly told me all he knew about it.

An Irish family by the name of Carroll came over from one of the Southern counties of Ireland and lived in a house on Wall Street where Hardin's Hall is now. They were Dan Carroll, his sisters, Mrs. Dunn, and Peggy—and a nephew, Dick Eagan. Dan Carroll was a tailor by trade and opened a tailor shop above the building now occupied by Hamilton's Book Store and Robinson's. His partner was Mr. West. They successfully operated their tailor shop until it was burned and, then they moved above Yardley, Wylie & Argur's Store, which is now Wylie & CO. and Artis Grocery. Shortly after the Civil War a soldier dropped off here after meeting the widow, Mrs. Dunn. They were married and had a son. Miss Peggy never married. Dan Carroll died a few years later. His family were devoted Catholics, and since Chester had no Catholic cemetery, they buried Dan in a secluded spot, which is now a part of Wylie Park. Dick Eagan the nephew, inherited all of his property.

I enjoyed every minute of my chat with Mr. Lathan. He will soon be 97 and has a remarkable memory and a great store of knowledge of Chester and Chester County. I asked him if he ever came in contact with Sherman during the war. He told me of the time he came home from the war and discovered that Sherman and his army had passed through his father's plantation on this famous march from Georgia. He said he saw no living thing as he came in sight of his home, not even the dog with his usual welcome. His father met him at the door and they sat on the steps while his father told him of the devastation Sherman and his soldiers wrought upon their farm. When word came that the army was coming the elder Mr. Lathan hurriedly filled their two horse wagon with corn and piled fodder on top, thinking the soldiers wouldn't bother a wagon seemingly filled with fodder. This he pulled away to the field. He hid a side of bacon and a sack of flour in a closet under the stairs and turned out all the animals. When Sherman's soldiers arrived they collected all the live stock except one small mule and five sheep that had wandered too far away. They slept on the cotton and burned it after their night's rest, also burned the wagon with the fodder. The soldiers poured out all of the sorghum that they couldn't eat and destroyed everything in sight, but did not discover the side of bacon, the sack of flour, a patch of potatoes, and a patch of wheat. When marching away one of the soldiers attracted by the dog barking at them, raised his Yankee rifle and shot the innocent dog.

Mr. Lathan said that in later years he used to sit in the barber shop and listen to men complain enough in fifteen minutes to last a lifetime. But just to think of the people back in those days facing a winter with practically nothing to live on. Some without homes. The wheat had to be saved to sell and plant so they ate bread made out of potatoes. Game was plentiful so they often enjoyed barbecue squirrel and rabbit. Later when berries ripened, berry pies with potato bread crusts were really good. The boys picked enough good seed out of the partly burned cotton to plant two acres. Out of the thirty bushels of wheat they sold ten bushels at $2.00 each. The rest was kept for planting and making flour. The cotton was sold at 23 ½ cents a pound. He remembered one bale, which brought $150.00 in gold. So with Mr. S. B. Lathan teaching school that first winter to buy clothes for the family and with the little they managed to save after Sherman's army left, they had a start toward a new beginning.

Mr. Lathan said that one of Mr. John Kennedy's daughters, who lived where the City Hall is now told him of Aaron Burr's trip through Chester. You remember Aaron Burr, a brilliant man who entered Princeton at the age of 12, to study law and continue to do so until the outbreak of the American Revolution. He joined the American Army and accompanied General Arnold in the latter's expedition toward Quebec. During the terrible ordeal of the journey through the wilderness he acquitted himself with great courage. On his arrival at Quebec, he was appointed Aide to General Montgomery. In 1776 he joined General Washington's military services but was soon dismissed for his dissipated habits, and for this he never forgave Washington. Being a very ambitious man he decided to set up a kingdom in the west and become ruler but was arrested in 1807 on a charge of treason. On the way to Richmond—an arrested man—he made his trip through Chester. John Kennedy's daughter saw them coming up the hill around nine o'clock one morning and was attracted by their uniforms. They stopped in front of Fowler Kennedy's Boarding House on top of the hill. A crowd soon gathered around. Mr. Burr got off his horse, looked frantically over the crowd and said, "I am the father-in-law of Governor Alston, and I am under military arrest. I claim civil protection." The sergeant quickly gathered him up, threw him back on his horse, and started hastily out Saluda street toward Lewis, known as Walker's then. They stopped for breakfast at Abram Smith's Boarding House, the Jones home now. After breakfast, while the horses were eating, Mr. Burr sat in they yard and leaned back on the root of a tree. He pulled his cap down over his eyes and sat there in silence. The lieutenant sent back to Chester for a gig, and last they saw of Aaron Burr he and the lieutenant were driving down the road. Later in Richmond his case was thrown out of court.

I'm sure most of us on our vacation trips to Myrtle Beach have visited lovely Brookgreen Gardens, which are now the great attraction of Brookgreen Plantation. This was the home of Theodosia, lovely wife of Governor Alston and only daughter of Aaron Burr. She was very fond of her father and often visited him in New York. On one of these visits her boat was lost and no one every heard of her again. Whether she was captured by pirates or lost at sea still remains a mystery.

Mr. Lathan told me of the first literary society in Chester and several other items of interest that I will tell you about next week.

Historical Sketches Of Chester County

The Chester Reporter

How Various Communities Got Their Names and Other Facts of Interest About Them as Related to a Reporter Representative By Dr. S. B. Lathan

By Catherine Irwin

When the Columbia-Charlotte railroad was built, in addition to depots, stations were located about every six miles which were called turnouts. These were built for the convenience of patrons of the road in shipping products. These turnouts were generally designated by the name of someone living in the neighborhood or owning property where they were located. About seven miles north of the city of Chester there was located one of these stations then named John Lewis Turn Out, now Lewis. The station was named for one, John Lewis, who was a civil engineer on the road. Originally the place was known as Walker's. Before the Court House was established in Chester, this section was known as Craven county. For the convenience of the citizens there were established in different sections what was known as county courts. One of these was presided over by a Mr. Walker. Around this place there sprang up a village and it was also a stopping place for the stage line that plied between Salisbury, North Carolina and Columbia, South Carolina. There was also located here what was known as a tavern which entertained passengers on the stagecoach for meals and lodging. Mr. Walker ran a store and a farm which was a great resort for neighboring farmers and others to congregate and gossip on the news of the day.

In the surrounding country there abounded at that time wild deer. Hunting these was the general sport of the well to do in the neighborhood. Fox hunting was unknown at this time, but many people kept hounds to hunt deer. Then, as now, a hound story was never questioned. Among these hunters there were three men who were particularly fond of the sport. They were Lewis Beckham, Thomas Chisholm, and James Crawford. One day while gossiping at Walker's store about their exploits, James Crawford told the story recapping while walking through his cornfield he spied a coon sitting about twenty-five feet up a post. He called his favorite hound, "Jack," patted him on the head and pointed to the coon up the tree. Jack made a bound, ran up the tree, caught the coon, jumped down with it in his mouth, and killed it. In April of the following year these three men were out in the surrounding territory deer hunting. Suddenly there came up a terrific thunderstorm. The hunters dismounted and stood silently holding their horses. Every moment they expected to be struck by lightning. After some time Crawford broke the silence, saying, "Boys, that was all a lie-that tale about Jack killing the coon."

Officers were carrying Aaron Burr to Richmond to be tried for treason. After their escapade in Chester they stopped in at Lewis and took breakfast at the tavern, then run by Mr. Abe Smith. After breakfast while the horses were being fed, Burr went out in the yard, sat down at the root of a tree, leaned back with his head against the trunk pulled the cap over his face and took a short nap. During the whole time that he was there he spoke not a single word. It is said that this was the only time in his life that Aaron Burr ever seemed to be "Cowed."

Besides these taverns and inns, kept for entertainment, a great many families entertained travelers, particularly married couples, who preferred private houses to taverns. On one occasion and a woman traveling in a carriage stopped at a Mr. McCullough's to spend the night. The next day the man said that he was going to New York to buy goods. The woman, he claimed as his wife, was unwell and had decided to remain until he returned for her. This was agreed to by Mr. and Mrs. McCullough. The trip would consume two or three months' time. In the interim the lady was encouched and brought forth a male child. One morning about two months after the birth of the child, after dressing her baby and putting him to sleep, the lady told Mrs. McCullough she was going down to the spring to wash out some of the child's laundry. About two hours later, the child awoke and Mrs. McCullough went to call the mother. Receiving no reply, she went to the spring, not finding her there and fearing misfortune, she called in several of the neighbors. They searched until late in the afternoon and found no clues. Finally Mrs. McCullough was informed by one of the neighbors that that morning about 10 o'clock he had seen a carryall parked at the side of the road near the spring and a lady get into it and go off with a man. That was the last they ever saw of the man and woman.

Mr. and Mrs. McCullough kept the child and reared it as if it were their own. A short time later they received a letter containing a nice sum of money with the request that the child be well cared for. As the boy grew older he was sent money with the request that he be sent to the best schools and when ready to enter college that he be sent to South Carolina College. Money was sent every year to fully meet all these expenses, but these letters could never be traced, for they were never mailed twice from the same place.

They came from Charleston, Richmond, New Orleans, Cincinnati and various other places. After graduation the boy read law in Chester, under John Mills, and became a full-fledged lawyer. Up until this time he did not know but that he was the son of the McCullough's, but one day an evil disposed person told him that he was not the McCullough's son, but a waif. After that he went to Mr. McCullough and inquired of him the facts of the case. McCullough tried to evade the question, but finally admitted the truth. After that the boy became despondent and gave up his flourishing law business, deterring if possible to find who his parents were. He left Chester and was last heard of in North Carolina. Whether he ever solved the mystery or not, remains unknown.

"Sadly, I was only one when my grandfather died"...however, I was fortunate to spend many hours visiting with my Aunt Susie and creating my own version of the portrait of Samuel Boston Lathan.

Section Four

A Willingness to Help

Acknowledgements

Sources and Acknowledgments

Fetters, Thomas. *Charleston and Hamburg, A South Carolina Railroad and American Legacy*. Charleston, SC: The History Press. 2008

Lathan, Rev. Robert, D.D. *History of South Carolina*. Atlanta, GA.: Wings Publishers. 2002

Lathan, William C.: Lathan archivist and personal communications.. Galax, VA.

Miles, Suzannah Smith. Research on Mount Pleasant, SC and personal communications. Charleston, SC.

Moore, George Harvey and Hartley, JoAnn. *The Lathan Legacy*. Charleston, SC.: The History Press. 2008

Priest, John Michael. *Before Antietam, The Battle for South Mountain*. Shippensburg, PA.: White Mane Publishing Co. 1992

Seigler, Robert S. M.D. *South Carolina's Military Organizations During the War Between the States*. Charleston, SC: The History Press. 2008

Welch, Leila Caldwell Stroud. *My Caldwell-Lathan Family Heritage*. 1999.